PINTS AND PATHWAYS

CONWAY
Bloomsbury Publishing Plc
50 Bedford Square, London, WC1B 3DP, UK
Bloomsbury Publishing Ireland Limited
29 Earlsfort Terrace, Dublin 2, Ireland

BLOOMSBURY, CONWAY and the Conway logo are trademarks of Bloomsbury Publishing Plc

First published in 2025

Copyright © Jacob Little, 2025
Photography © Jacob Little, except where otherwise stated on page 238
Maps: Ordnance Survey Maps © Crown copyright and database rights, 2024, OS AC0000852561

Jacob Little has asserted his right under the Copyright, Designs and Patents Act, 1988, to be identified as Author of this work

For legal purposes the Acknowledgements on page 238 constitute an extension of this copyright page

This book is a guide for when you spend time outdoors. Undertaking any activity outdoors carries with it some risks that cannot be entirely eliminated. For example, you might get lost on a route or caught in bad weather. Before you spend time outdoors, we therefore advise that you always take the necessary precautions, such as checking weather forecasts and ensuring that you have all the equipment you need. Any walking routes that are described in this book should not be relied upon as a sole means of navigation, so we recommend that you refer to an Ordnance Survey map or authoritative equivalent.

This book may also reference businesses and venues. Whilst every effort is made by the author and the publisher to ensure the accuracy of the business and venue information contained in our books before they go to print, changes to such information can occur during the production and lifetime of a publication. Therefore, we also advise that you check with businesses or venues for the latest information before setting out.

All internet addresses given in this book were correct at the time of going to press. Bloomsbury Publishing Plc does not have any control over, or responsibility for, any third-party websites referred to or in this book. The author and the publisher regret any inconvenience caused if some facts have changed or sites have ceased to exist, but can accept no responsibility for any such changes.

All rights reserved. No part of this publication may be: i) reproduced or transmitted in any form, electronic or mechanical, including photocopying, recording or by means of any information storage or retrieval system without prior permission in writing from the publishers; or ii) used or reproduced in any way for the training, development or operation of artificial intelligence (AI) technologies, including generative AI technologies. The rights holders expressly reserve this publication from the text and data mining exception as per Article 4(3) of the Digital Single Market Directive (EU) 2019/790

A catalogue record for this book is available from the British Library
Library of Congress Cataloguing-in-Publication data has been applied for
ISBN: 978-1-8448-6667-0; eBook: 978-1-8448-6668-7; ePDF: 978-1-8448-6666-3

2 4 6 8 10 9 7 5 3 1

Typeset in Adobe Caslon Pro by Phil Beresford
Printed and bound in India by Replika Press Pvt. Ltd.

To find out more about our authors and books visit www.bloomsbury.com and sign up for our newsletters
For product safety related questions contact productsafety@bloomsbury.com

PINTS AND PATHWAYS

50 SCENIC WALKS TO THE PUBS OF RURAL ENGLAND

Jacob Little

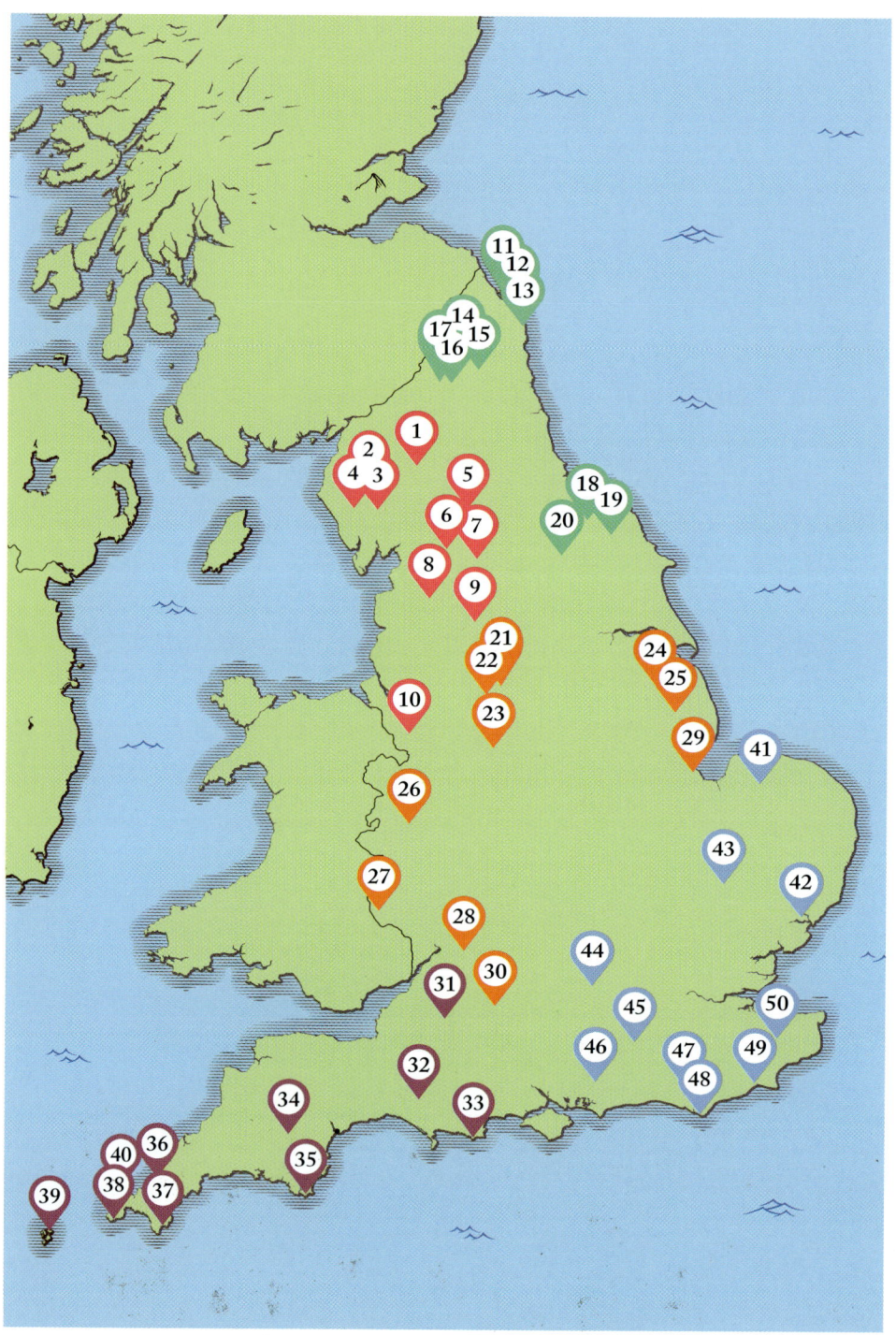

CONTENTS

Introduction 9
How to use this guide 13

NORTH-WEST

1 Greg's Hut, Cross Fell & The Shepherds Inn 16
2 Black Moss Pot from Stonethwaite & The Langstrath Country Inn 20
3 Loughrigg Tarn & The Britannia Inn 24
4 Scafell Pike from Wasdale Head & Wasdale Head Inn 28
5 Keld and Ravenseat & Tan Hill Inn 33
6 Ribblehead Viaduct & The Station Inn 37
7 Great Whernside & The Blue Bell Inn 41
8 The Ribble Valley & The Inn at Whitewell 45
9 Hebden Bridge & Pack Horse Inn 50
10 Sandstone Trail & The Pheasant Inn 54

NORTH-EAST

11 Holy Island Circular & The Ship Inn 60
12 Seahouses to Bamburgh Circular & The Olde Ship Inn 64
13 Craster, Dunstanburgh Castle, Low Newton-by-the-Sea & The Ship Inn 68
14 Alwin River & The Rose and Thistle 72
15 The Drake Stone at Harbottle & The Star Inn 76
16 Greenhaugh Circular & Holly Bush Inn 80
17 Kielder Forest & The Pheasant Inn 85
18 Blakey Ridge, Rosedale Railway & The Lion Inn 89
19 Hole of Horcum & The Horseshoe Inn 93
20 Kilburn White Horse & The Fauconberg 97

CENTRAL & NORTHERN

21 Edale Circular & The Old Nags Head 104
22 Bugsworth Basin & The Old Hall Inn 108
23 Cauldon & Yew Tree Inn 112
24 Tealby Loop & The Kings Head 117
25 Lincolnshire Wolds & The Blue Bell Inn 121
26 Caer Caradoc & The Royal Oak 125
27 Black Hill & The Bull's Head 129
28 Slad Valley & The Woolpack Inn 135
29 Fotheringhay, Elton & The Falcon Inn 138
30 Avebury, Silbury Hill & The Red Lion 142

SOUTH-WEST

31 South Stoke Circular & The Packhorse 148
32 The Melbury Park Estate & The Acorn Inn 152
33 Worth Matravers, Winspit Quarry & The Square and Compass 156
34 Dartmoor & The Warren House Inn 160
35 Prawle Head & Pigs Nose Inn 165
36 St Agnes Beacon & The Driftwood Spars 169
37 The Serpentine Circular & The Cadgwith Cove Inn 173
38 Logan Rock, Porth Chapel, Gwennap Head & The Logan Rock Inn ... 177
39 St Martin's, Isles of Scilly & The Seven Stones Inn 182
40 Zennor Head Circular & The Tinners Arms 186

SOUTH-EAST

41 Helhoughton, Raynham & Sculthorpe Mill 192
42 Pin Mill & The Butt & Oyster 196
43 Devil's Dyke & The Three Blackbirds 200
44 Hambleden, Pheasant's Hill & The Stag & Huntsman 204
45 Shere & The White Horse 209
46 Beacon Hill & The Three Horseshoes 213
47 Firle Beacon & The Ram Inn 217
48 Birling Gap, Beachy Head & The Tiger Inn 221
49 Rye & The Playden Oasts Inn 226
50 Down Wood from Chilham & The White Horse Inn 230

Acknowledgements 234
Index 235

INTRODUCTION

What makes a good pub? You may say good food, good service, great beer or excellent wine. You may also mention décor, amenities, good facilities and a buzzing atmosphere.

There is no doubt all these things matter. They are all features of the pubs we want to visit, and within the pages of this book, you will find a selection of places that match all these criteria. However, the history of England and our rural landscape tells us that there's much more to a good pub that stands the test of time.

Within the walls of some of these historic buildings, stories have been conjured, told and retold. The most inspiring books have been written, some of England's defining political moments have played out, and vital deals have been brokered that have set our country's path and helped define how we view ourselves today. A good pub is, by its very nature, democratising; any other building with such history is normally behind a façade of protection that deems access is only possible for a chosen few. Pubs are for everyone and have, for centuries, provided a space to speak a common language.

In *Pints and Pathways*, you will find a selection of walks to pubs viewed within the context of their geography, and the communities they serve. Whether that's a pub watching over a historic fishing community (see page 172), or one that served as lodging for railway workers building one of the most impressive Victorian engineering projects in the country (see page 37), there's a mixture of landscapes, histories, communities and industries within the pages of this book. From the isolated and windswept north-east to the rolling hills of the south-east, each of these landscapes has its own character, and their pubs have their own traditions and conventions. I hope some of this is captured here.

The walks included are often circular, passing through nearby towns and villages, and by experiencing these pubs as part of their backdrop, I hope it allows you to appreciate the toil behind each patch of farmland, the bravery of each person down every mine and on each fishing boat – and the hard-fought livelihoods that are won and lost across generations.

There is also a modern story to tell. Pubs today need support. Experts say that in the first half of 2024, on average 50 pubs shut each month. These closures not only deprive landlords of employment, but also communities of their shared space; a space that is their own and one where stories and a generational understanding of landscape can be passed down. Perhaps

◄ Locals enjoying at lunchtime pint at the Holly Bush Inn, Greenhaugh

▲ A roaring fire at The Packhorse Pub, in South Stoke, near Bath (see page 148).

by looking at our much-celebrated pubs through the lens of what we might end up losing, we can tell a compelling story about how pubs offer an opportunity to reconnect to places, people and landscapes. We know that this connection is something many of us long for today.

The walks in this book are also intended to raise a glass to our English countryside in all its diverse glory, and there are walks here that I hope will provide inspiration to strap on your hiking boots and spend quality time with friends, family and loved ones. These are 50 of my favourite walks, but there could so easily be 5,000 – perhaps the beauty of England's rural land is that I will have missed many, many great walks and great pubs, and that part of the joy is in one's own exploration. In the meantime, I hope this provides a good starting point and an enjoyable complement to a great local pint.

▶ The hidden, winding paths that link communities and their pubs are celebrated throughout this book.

INTRODUCTION

HOW TO USE THIS GUIDE

*P*ints and Pathways is divided into five different sections, one for each region of England, from the north-west and north-east, down through the centre of the country to the south-east and south-west. Within each regional section, walks are then grouped by proximity to one another, and many of these walks can be completed in a relatively short period, allowing you to make the most of your time and get under the skin of a location during a short break or weekend. If you find yourself looking for something to do in a particular area, then turn to that section of book; it's likely there's a lovely walk near you.

There is something for everyone in this book. I realise it's often not easy, convenient or always possible to hike up big mountains on full-day treks – although I have included a few of those walks. Rather, this book largely comprises morning and afternoon strolls; walks that can be completed in half a day or less, with a good pint or a pub lunch to start or end your day and routes that consider the highlights and history of the surrounding areas.

▼ Descending from Great Whernside in the Yorkshire Dales.

It's worth mentioning that I am indebted to generations of hikers and ramblers who have not only provided inspiration for this book, but have also mapped much of this land over years of treading the pathways between communities. This book doesn't set out or claim to reinvent any of these routes, many of which have undoubtedly been printed many times before.

This is a celebration, collection and compendium of trails, a handy reference to inspire your research, investigation and understanding of the communities behind each pub that are themselves inexorably linked to the geography in which they sit.

For each pub walk, I have included a panel of information that provides at-a-glance information about the walk. Distance and elevation data will give you an idea of the walk's difficulty, and the start and end point (often the pubs that you'll return to) can be customised depending on available parking; I have included Ordnance Survey maps in this guide so you can follow the route, get an idea of the surrounding terrain and understand what amenities are in the vicinity.

Where available, I have also included details of the nearest bus stop or train station. Many of these walks, although centred in rural areas, are near larger towns or cities, so planning a car-free visit is entirely possible. I'd recommend looking at journey-planning websites, such as Rome2Rio.com or Traveline.info, if you intend to complete these pub walks via public transport. These websites offer bus and train timetables

▲ The grand dining hall of The Old Hall Inn, Chinley (see page 108).

and consider transport changes, time to walk between locations and which websites you should visit to purchase tickets and get up-to-date travel information.

I've also provided websites for the pubs in question, many of which have accessibility information included on their site, as well as opening times, menus and booking options.

HOW TO USE THIS GUIDE

NORTH-WEST

There are few places in England where natural beauty, industrial history and cultural richness intertwine as seamlessly as they do in the north-west. Many of the walks here focus on enjoying the raw beauty of this area's geography, with the Lake District standing as its crown jewel. The dramatic peaks, glittering lakes and deep valleys of the Lakes have inspired poets, painters and wanderers for centuries.

To the east, the Pennines rise, often referred to as the 'backbone of England'. This range of hills stretches across the region, creating a natural boundary between the north-west and north-east of the country. Walks up Cross Fell (see page 16) and the the uplands around Britain's highest pub, Tan Hill Inn (see page 33), are some of the best routes to enjoy sweeping, panoramic views across remote expanses of wilderness. Yet, just a short distance away, the scenery shifts dramatically to the industrial heartlands of Lancashire and Greater Manchester. Here, towering chimneys of old cotton mills stand as monuments to a time when the north-west was the engine of the world. Canals, once vital arteries of the Industrial Revolution, crisscross the area that was once filled with the hum of factories and the rhythm of working life.

It was indeed the Industrial Revolution that transformed the north-west into a powerhouse of innovation and production. Cities grew rapidly and the area's urban

centres thrived, bringing prosperity, but also hardship, for many as the population swelled. On the coast, Liverpool played a crucial role in Britain's maritime history. As one of the world's greatest ports, it was a gateway to the British Empire, its docks bustling with ships transporting goods to and from every corner of the globe. Many of these industrial spaces; ports, canals, old mills and factories have found new life, transformed into cultural spaces and museums, breathing new life into the region's heritage.

In rural areas, particularly in the counties of Cumbria and Lancashire, ancient customs like Morris dancing, fell running and local fairs continue to thrive, with strong, resilient communities preserving their distinct sense of identity and culture. Over time, many areas in the north-west have reinvented themselves as centres for music, art and media, and the post-industrial landscape has, over the latter stages of the 20th century and into the 21st, become fertile ground for creativity.

Though the mills may have fallen silent years ago, the walks in this region celebrate the industrial power and might of its past, complemented by welcoming pubs that showcase the best of British hospitality. Local beers and award-winning cuisine, made from the area's abundant produce, are a fitting end to a day spent exploring this fascinating region.

1

GREG'S HUT, CROSS FELL & THE SHEPHERDS INN

— 15.3km (9.5 miles) —

One of the most impressive walks in northern England, and one of my favourites anywhere in the country, this walk is designed for hikers who want a test. Its length, the scale of the ascent and the dramatic landscape in which it sits means that this walk is best enjoyed by competent hill walkers only. For most of us with a good pair of walking boots and adequate supplies for a long day out, it's a rewarding hike to the heart of the remote North Pennines region.

Located in the Eden Valley, the red sandstone buildings of Langwathby provide a good base for this walk. To start, drive the small lanes towards Skirwith and Blencarn. If you want an additional challenge, you can also walk from The Shepherds Inn at Langwathby, but be prepared for lots of lane walking before you get to the start of the climb.

THE WALK

From Langwathby, drive towards Skirwith village and on towards the tiny farming hamlet of Kirkland. At the road's end, there's a parking spot (which we'll return to later) with space for a small number of cars.

Begin the ascent of Cross Fell by taking a track that is well-marked and starts off as a gravel road before turning into a grassy path. If you're ever in doubt as to where to go, follow the signs for the Pennine Way. The initial climb is

▶ The view from the warm shelter of Greg's Hut.

THE PUB: The Shepherds Inn, Langwathby Bridge, Langwathby, Penrith, Cumbria CA10 1LW
www.shepherds-inn.co.uk
01768 881463

START AND END POINT: Kirkland, Penrith, Cumbria CA10 1RN

WALK LENGTH: 15.3km (9.5 miles)

ASCENT: 781m (2,562ft)

APPROX. TIME: 4 hours 30 minutes

PARKING: A small parking area is available in Kirkland, at the beginning of the ascent to Cross Fell

CAR FREE: Village Green bus stop available in Blencarn, 1.6km (1 mile) away from the start of the walk

gentle, but it becomes steeper as you approach the summit and can be boggy in places. As you climb, you'll pass several old stone walls and sheepfolds, reminders that this has been working land for many generations.

At 893m (2,930ft), Cross Fell is the highest point in both the Pennine Range and in England outside the Lake District. On a clear day, you can see westward to northern England's 'bigger brother', and to the north, you can see the Solway Firth of Scotland and its southern hills.

The name 'Cross Fell' is believed to have evolved from the Old Norse word *krossa*, meaning 'cross', which reflects the cross-shaped cairns that were historically erected by monks from the nearby abbeys during the medieval period to mark their boundaries and provide navigational aids in the frequent foggy conditions. Later, during the 18th and 19th centuries, the fell and its surrounding areas were extensively mined for lead and silver. You can still see remnants of this mining activity, such as old mine shafts and spoil heaps.

From the summit of Cross Fell, continue north along the Pennine Way, until the path descends steeply before levelling out at Greg's Hut. As the highest and one of the most remote bothies in England, Greg's Hut is maintained by the Mountain Bothies Association (MBA) and used by walkers, local shepherds and, on occasion, the Penrith Mountain Rescue Team. This former miner's cottage, offering basic – and sometimes lifesaving – shelter, was named in

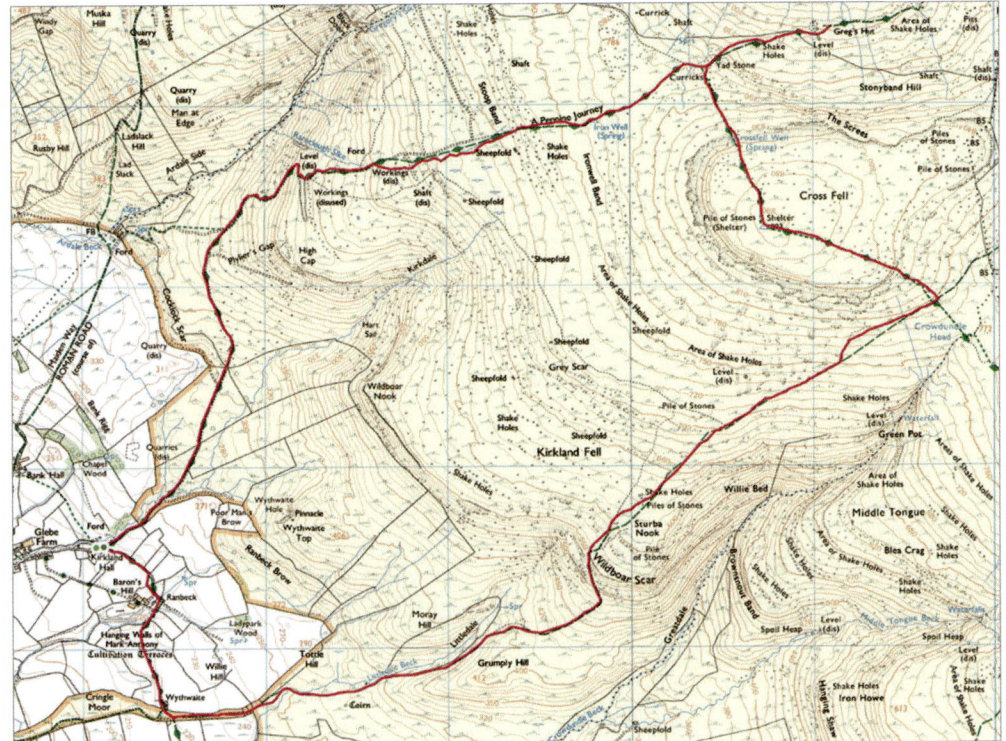

memory of John Gregory, a keen walker and MBA member who died in a climbing accident in the Alps in 1968. It has become a vital stop for walkers traversing the Pennine Way.

From Greg's Hut, go back the way you came and instead of going back down Cross Fell, turn left and on to Little Dun Fell and Great Dun Fell, two slightly smaller peaks. From a distance, you'll notice some celestial objects on the horizon – Great Dun Fell is home to a radar station, which is a key part of the Air Traffic Control system in Scotland and northern England, a surveillance radar and a permanent meteorological observatory. Continue along the Pennine Way about halfway to Little Dun Fell. At Tees Head, turn right and begin your descent downhill, following the route down Wildboar Scar as you start the return leg of your walk. Once you're at the bottom, follow the path round to the right at Wythwaite and on to Kirkland Hall and the car parking spaces. From here, drive the short distance back to the pub at Langwathby, enjoying a pint on the generous village green.

◀ Greg's Hut is a former mining cottage and now provides welcome relief for workers and walkers in this unforgiving environment.

NORTH-WEST

2

BLACK MOSS POT FROM STONETHWAITE & THE LANGSTRATH COUNTRY INN

— 6.4km (4 miles) —

Between numerous high peaks in the Lake District sit pools that have been carved out of the rock by centuries of flowing water. Many of these are now well-known as wild swimming destinations, and some are easily accessible, offering opportunities to dip into ice-cold water during the hotter seasons when hiking here can be gruelling and unforgiving.

Black Moss Pot is one such haven, tucked away within the heart of the remote and rugged beauty of the Langstrath Valley. Nestled between towering hillsides, the pool is fed by a small but forceful waterfall. The water here is an almost mystical shade of dark green, so deep it appears black in the shadows, giving the pot its name. The air here is crisp and cool, carrying with it an earthy scent. The stillness is only broken by the occasional cry

of a distant bird, or the soft bleating of sheep that graze on the hillsides above. During busier months, you'll be sharing this spot with a few other intrepid swimmers, but it's a wonderful place to stay a while and there's flat ground close by making it an excellent stop-off point. The nearby village of Stonethwaite is picture-perfect Lake District, plus it boasts an excellent pub that makes a great start and end point to this walk.

THE WALK

Framed by rugged hills and verdant hillsides, the stone cottages of Stonethwaite are tightly nestled together in the valley of the Stonethwaite Beck. Situated on the Cumbria Way long-distance footpath, there are excellent accommodation options here, including a YHA and a large campsite with views across the neighbouring hillsides.

From The Langstrath Country Inn, turn left and immediately through the gate into a field that marks the start of the walk to Black Moss Pot. It's an easy, well-trodden and well-surfaced path that subsequently leads you through to another gate on the opposite side of the field – continue along the path, keeping the river on your left. The path follows the beck (common word for 'stream' in this part of northern England) closely, and the fells rise steeply on either side – in summer they're often covered with a carpet of purple heather.

After a couple of kilometres on this path, and before the path curves around to the right into the valley, you'll come across Galleny Force, a series of small but beautiful waterfalls and pools, and a spot that's also popular for a quick rest or a refreshing dip, with the water cascading into clear, deep pools surrounded by mossy boulders.

After leaving Galleny Force, the path becomes a bit rougher and less defined as you follow the beck upstream, around to the right and into the valley. The valley narrows here and the hillsides become steeper as the walk funnels you towards Black Moss Pot. The walking is easy, but it can be rough underfoot. Look out for Eagle Crag with the beck on your left and the high sides of the fells either side of you.

Black Moss Pot is a striking sight, initially a bit hidden from the path at the bottom of a deep, natural pit carved into the rock by centuries of water erosion. The beck tumbles into the pool from above, creating a deep section of water surrounded by smooth stone walls, enclosed by steep cliffsides with hardy trees clinging to the rocks.

◂ Walking towards Black Moss Pot, you'll be spoilt by a stunning example of a Lake District valley.

Although it's a popular spot, the area around Black Moss Pot is wild and untamed, with bracken-covered hillsides and scattered boulders that were dropped haphazardly by an ancient glacier.

Take a moment to sit on one of the large, flat rocks beside the pot, listening to the sounds of nature and taking in the view. When you're ready to leave, you can retrace your steps back through the Langstrath Valley to Stonethwaite and The Langstrath Country Inn.

Built in the 16th century as a miner's cottage, the inn is a small family-run sanctuary for walkers and has been extended to host 11 comfortable bedrooms, as well as its own fenced garden. It has the added benefit of being situated on two famous walking routes – Wainwright's Coast to Coast and the Cumbrian Way – so if you're staying in the area a little longer, this is a great base.

◄ Many of the walks in these areas are framed by lovely examples of stone walls.

► It's cold, but taking a dip in Black Moss Pot can provide welcome relief after a day's hiking.

THE PUB: The Langstrath Country Inn, Stonethwaite, Keswick, Cumbria CA12 5XG
www.thelangstrath.co.uk
01768 777239

START AND END POINT: The Langstrath Country Inn (see above)

WALK LENGTH: 6.4km (4 miles)

ASCENT: 101m (331ft)

APPROX. TIME: 1 hour 30 minutes

PARKING: Village car parking available by the red telephone box in Stonethwaite, near the pub

CAR FREE: Stonethwaite Road End bus stop for buses to/from Keswick

3

LOUGHRIGG TARN & THE BRITANNIA INN

— 9.2km (5.7 miles) —

Although the village of Elterwater became central to the Lake District's tourism boom in the early 20th century, there's still a slightly more 'out the way' feel here. It's located a little way out of the popular town of Ambleside, with the 19th-century Britannia Inn sitting at the heart of the village that is at the eastern edge of the impressive Great Langdale valley. On good weather days, the valley's position is so favourable and its peaks so high, that you may find the Royal Air Force or United States Air Force practising their low-level flying from nearby bases. The occasional sight and sound of fighter jets accompanying your day out makes this location all the more dramatic.

THE WALK

Start at the front door of The Britannia Inn and turn left, back towards the main road. At the road, cross over and begin the ascent on a small lane, past a café on your left, up towards Huntingstile Crag. There are plenty of options to take shortcuts on this route up, which is especially useful if the road is busy with passing traffic.

Continue on the road as it ascends until you reach a sharp series of turns – you will carry on here, passing YHA Langdale on your right, a Victorian mansion and three-tier arboretum at High Close, which is managed by the National Trust. High Close Garden itself has over 1,000 years of fascinating history and is home to many rare trees and shrubs from all around the globe. The Trust-run tree trail is worth a look for budding arborists.

You'll go downhill at this point after leaving the hostel behind you, and enter through the gates on the right, routing into Redbank Wood. Go through the woods and you'll soon emerge onto Loughrigg Terrace with Ewe Crag above you. There are two options here, and you'll come back onto the terrace later, but for now take the right set of steep steps that head upwards towards the Loughrigg summit. It's a moderately challenging climb, but well worth it for the variety of different views on offer once you reach the top; almost always spectacular no matter what the weather. Look out onto the imposing Langdale Pikes, and south towards Lake Windermere.

The way down is gentler, as you take a permissive path on the other side of the summit that descends via Rydal Water and the disused quarry that forms the basis of the Rydal Caves – a small detour but well worth it. The going can be marshy and boggy here, and instead of the lush, verdant greens in the area around Loughrigg Terrace, it feels more ancient and wilder, with ferns and water-loving species all around you. As you head down this path, you'll also get a great view of Rydal Water spanning out in front of you.

You'll soon pass through areas of woodland and open land, with the path becoming more defined as you approach the Lake. Before reaching Rydal Water, look for a signpost directing you back towards Elterwater. This path will lead you towards more woodland. Just

before you reach this, turn down a slope towards the water and a little beach on the most southerly edge of Grasmere. Here you'll find people picnicking, dogs swimming and children playing; it's a great place to stop for a while.

Continue to the far edge of the beach area, turning left at the end, and retrace your route up through woods until you reach a sharp hill, which is the bottom of the road you turned right on earlier to enter Loughrigg Terrace. Turn left up the hill – watch for passing traffic – and climb up an area of woodland you descended into earlier. Before long, you'll reach the turning back to Elterwater – go right here, back past the YHA and onto the winding road that descends back to The Britannia Inn.

As well as enough passing trade to keep the pub busy, you'll meet a typical Lakeland scene here, with lovely worn stone walls, a slate roof and a handful of picnic benches outside. The pub

is keen to stay true to its roots and foster a sense of local community. It hosts quiz and music nights and there are also rooms to stay in if you'd like to base yourself here. It has historical connections to the slate industry, which was prominent in the area, and slate workers from nearby quarries would often visit the inn, making it an integral part of the local economy – there's lots of memorabilia on the walls. My tip is to sit with a pint and one of their hot filled rolls or naan breads; they have an excellent lunch menu to feed the feet of weary walkers.

> **THE PUB:** The Britannia Inn, Elterwater, Ambleside, Cumbria LA22 9HP
> www.thebritanniainn.com
> 015394 37210
>
> **START AND END POINT:** 4 Mill Row Car Park, Elterwater, Ambleside, Cumbria LA22 9HP
>
> **WALK LENGTH:** 9.2km (5.7 miles)
>
> **ASCENT:** 554m (1,818ft)
>
> **APPROX. TIME:** 2 hours 45 minutes
>
> **PARKING:** 4 Mill Row Car Park (see above)
>
> **CAR FREE:** The Britannia Inn bus stop for buses from Ambleside

▲ The Britannia Inn has a lovely Lakeland feel, with a great lunch menu and enough local beers to keep you entertained for an afternoon.

◄ Strolling along Loughrigg Terrace, with the dramatic landscape across the valley ahead.

4

SCAFELL PIKE FROM WASDALE HEAD & WASDALE HEAD INN

— 8.5km (5.3 miles) —

Like many journeys into the remote heartlands of the Lake District, getting to Wasdale Head is, in and of itself, an adventure. To get here, you'll skim the coastline of the western edge of the Lakes, before diverting inland at Gosforth and hugging the shoreline of Wast Water with looming peaks of Scafell, Kirk Fell and Great Gable in front of you.

The mountains here create a natural amphitheatre and, surrounded on three sides, you really feel nestled into the heart of the most dramatic Lakes geography. The most imposing peak here is Scafell Pike. At 978m (3,209ft), it is the highest mountain in England. Wasdale Head Inn serves as the gateway to Scafell Pike and this walk.

Attracting adventurers and outdoor enthusiasts from all over the world, you can expect this walk to be busy, but the sheer scale of the landscape here means that you'll always have moments to yourself. Should you wish for a quieter route, it is recommended to tackle this walk in the shoulder seasons. You'll also need ample outdoor gear and plenty of water and snacks, as well as a keen sense of mountain weather given how quickly it can change. If you have them, walking poles are highly recommended as the going is rocky, especially on the way down.

From Wasdale Head Inn, the most popular and straightforward route to Scafell Pike is via the Lingmell Gill path. This route is well-trodden and marked, making it accessible for those attempting the climb for the first time.

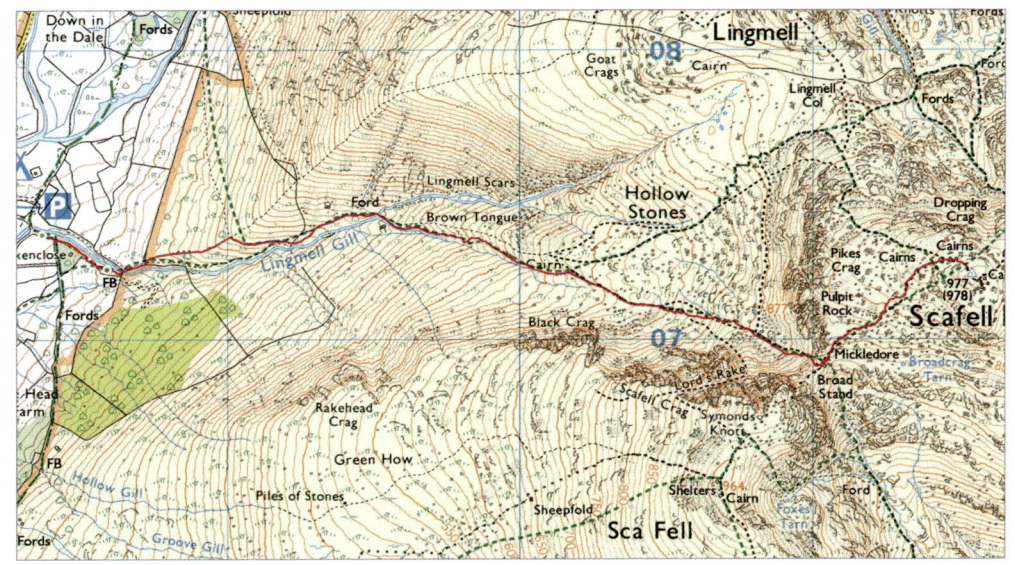

THE WALK

The journey begins at the Lakehead Car Park, which is free for National Trust members, or £9 for non-members to park all day. From here, follow the footpath along Lingmell Beck and cross the stone bridge over it, following the path that starts to ascend gently along Lingmell Gill. It's a relatively low-lying, easy walk here and the initial part of the journey offers a relatively easy gradient. The path hugs the right side of Lingmell Gill, which, although it stands in Scafell's shadow, is a separate fell that still sits at a relatively impressive 807m (2,648ft). The section of the walk that follows is a steady climb – the southern edge of the Gill is rounded and sloping, contrasting with the northern face, which boasts 300m (1,000ft) sheer drops to the valley floor. The landscape here is typically rugged Lakeland, with crags and boulders scattered across the terrain.

After about an hour of steady climbing, you'll reach a flatter area known as Hollow Stones. Many people use this spot to take a break and open the picnic, as the site offers splendid views back down the valley. The imposing bulk of Scafell Pike looms ahead, but by now you will be able to clearly see the route you need to take.

Leaving Hollow Stones, the path heads north-east and begins to steepen as it heads up towards Lingmell Col. The terrain becomes increasingly

NORTH-WEST

rocky and uneven here and it's at this point that fatigue may set in, although you'll be in good company.

Upon reaching Lingmell Col, you'll find a broad, flat saddle between the peaks of Lingmell and Scafell Pike. From here, the final ascent to the summit begins. The path may require some scrambling over loose rocks and there are several routes – most people will be heading to the summit, so you'll be with others, but be sure to turn right to reach the summit rather than join the Corridor Route that passes Great End. As you gain altitude, the views become more expansive, and in good weather these are some of the best mountain vistas anywhere in the country.

The summit is marked by a large cairn and a trig point. On a clear day, you'll be looking out as far as Scotland to the north, Wales to the south, and the Isle of Man to the west. On a good

▼ As a natural amphitheatre of some of the most impressive mountains anywhere in the country, this is a hill walker's paradise.

weather day stop for a break and take it all in – the climb is no small feat.

Returning to the pub, the safest and most straightforward route back is to retrace your steps down Lingmell Col and back along Lingmell Gill. Wasdale Head Inn has a long history of welcoming travellers back from scaling the peaks of the Lake District, and once you get back down,

THE PUB: Wasdale Head Inn, Wasdale Head, nr Gosforth, Cumbria CA20 1EX
🌐 www.wasdale.com
📞 01946 726229

START AND END POINT: Lake Head Car Park, Wasdale, Cumbria CA20 1EX

WALK LENGTH: 8.5km (5.3 miles)

ASCENT: 902m (2,959ft)

APPROX. TIME: 4 hours

PARKING: Lake Head Car Park (see above), or near Wasdale Head Inn at Lingmell House

CAR FREE: No suitable public transport, although the Wasdale Shuttle minibus runs seasonally from Ravenglass – check the website for more information: www.lakedistrict.gov.uk/visiting/getting-to-the-lake-district/wasdale-shuttlebus

it's worth taking a break here, as well as exploring the adjacent Barn Door Shop, which sells a variety of outdoor gear, maps and equipment. Often touted as the home of British climbing, Wasdale Head Inn played host to tourists during the golden age of climbing in England at the turn of the 20th century, when this new sport was invented by the thousands of visitors vacating the cities and enjoying the emergence of a now expansive transport system in England. The feeling is not too dissimilar today, and although it's one of the busiest and most popular walking routes anywhere in the country, it's also one of the most impressive.

▼ The Wasdale Head Inn has a history of welcoming walkers for many years, and there's a little outdoor shop next to it that's worth visiting.

5

KELD AND RAVENSEAT & TAN HILL INN

— 14km (8.7 miles) —

On one Friday in November 2021, pubgoers at Tan Hill Inn on the Yorkshire Dales were settling in for a cosy evening by the fire at England's highest pub. Over the course of the next three days, they'd find themselves at the heart of worldwide media headlines, as Storm Arwen quickly swept across the surrounding moorland.

Waking up to a metre (3ft) of snow surrounding the pub, everyone who was there on the Friday night ended up staying for the whole weekend, with the pub manager fielding calls from media agencies across the globe. Customers shared rooms, slept on the floor and occupied themselves by playing games and waiting for the snowploughs to arrive. When they finally did, three days later, firm friendships had been formed, and the group that was stuck there that winter have since revisited the pub for annual reunions.

The story is a tale of stoicism that matches the pub's defiant atmosphere. Tan Hill Inn sits sentinel on a patch of untamed wilderness surrounded by the most rugged parts of the Yorkshire Dales. Quite rightly, it's proud of its status as England's highest pub, and the building itself bears witness to its location; centuries of relentless winds and storms have taken its toll, but the rugged feel outside is equally matched with how comfortable and welcoming it feels inside.

Step out from the pub's fire-warmed embrace and the crisp, invigorating air of the moorland greets you, often carrying with it the scent of heather and peat during the warmer months. The vast, open sky is instantly noticeable, as is the weather. Moody, grey and foreboding skies are the norm here, but the best are those breezy blue-sky days, with puffs of white cloud that drift shadows across the landscape.

THE WALK

To start the walk, head right from the pub door and then immediately left onto the moorland. It's a clearly marked road and before long, when the path branches off at a sign, take the right turn and cross the moorland towards streams, which you'll ford, heading up towards the hillside on the opposite side. Climbing uphill, the path bears around to the left as you sit on top of Thomas Gill Hill and then Robert's Seat, continuing south across the wild moors. Through the fence line via a stile, you'll begin downhill into the valley, with Ravenseat below you.

Once you reach the bottom of the valley you ford a small beck and pass farm buildings, continuing along the waymarked route as the path bends round to the east, circling the West

▼ The regularly stoked, warming fire of the Tan Hill Inn is not just for decoration; it's a must to keep this pub warm and cosy, thanks to its remote location.

Stonesdale Out Pasture. Keeping the river on your right, look out for waterfalls as you walk. Keep left at Oven Mouth, a beck feeding water from the moorland into the river, and then continue on to the road at West Stonesdale, a couple of kilometres further along.

Once you've reached the road, you'll be greeted by a small farming hamlet, with little more here than working machinery, a red post box and an old telephone box – two solitary links from here to the outside world. Cross the lane and go through the field to the right of it, before descending away from the hamlet towards the Stonesdale Beck.

Follow the beck north with a small building identifiable on your right, known as Carr House, before the path gets a lot clearer as you join the Pennine Way on a small track leading to a B&B called Frith Lodge. After tramping across desolate and remote moorland, the rest of the walk feels comparatively easy-going thanks to the mostly well-defined path of the Pennine Way, as well as the other hikers you're likely to be sharing this route with by now. As you continue to meander north, look out over the vast vistas around you and consider what it takes to build a

---

THE PUB: Tan Hill Inn, Long Causeway, Richmond, N. Yorks DL11 6ED
🌐 www.tanhillinn.com
📞 01833 533007

START AND END POINT: Tan Hill Inn (see above)

WALK LENGTH: 14km (8.7 miles)

ASCENT: 392m (1,286ft)

APPROX. TIME: 3 hours 45 minutes

PARKING: Car park at Tan Hill Inn (see above), on the opposite side of the road

CAR FREE: Buses from Catterick Garrison stop in Keld, a short walk away from West Stonesdale, so it's possible to start there and incorporate a stop at Tan Hill Inn at the halfway mark

---

▼ Standing on a high patch of moorland, the highest pub in England comes complete with its own snow vehicles, and plenty of excellent walking opportunities.

community here – let alone an isolated pub and all the functioning elements of a successful remote agricultural system.

Once you're back at the pub, a good day's stomp will be met by a hearty gaggle of hikers, ramblers, climbers, runners and walkers, as well as plenty of bikers who often visit the pub on sorties around the moorland roads. Most of the time, the snowploughs that sit on either side of the pub's entrance are ready and waiting for their moment to shine, and are only needed during the bitterest of winters. That being said, if November 2021 is anything to go by, it might just be worth packing an extra woolly jumper or two.

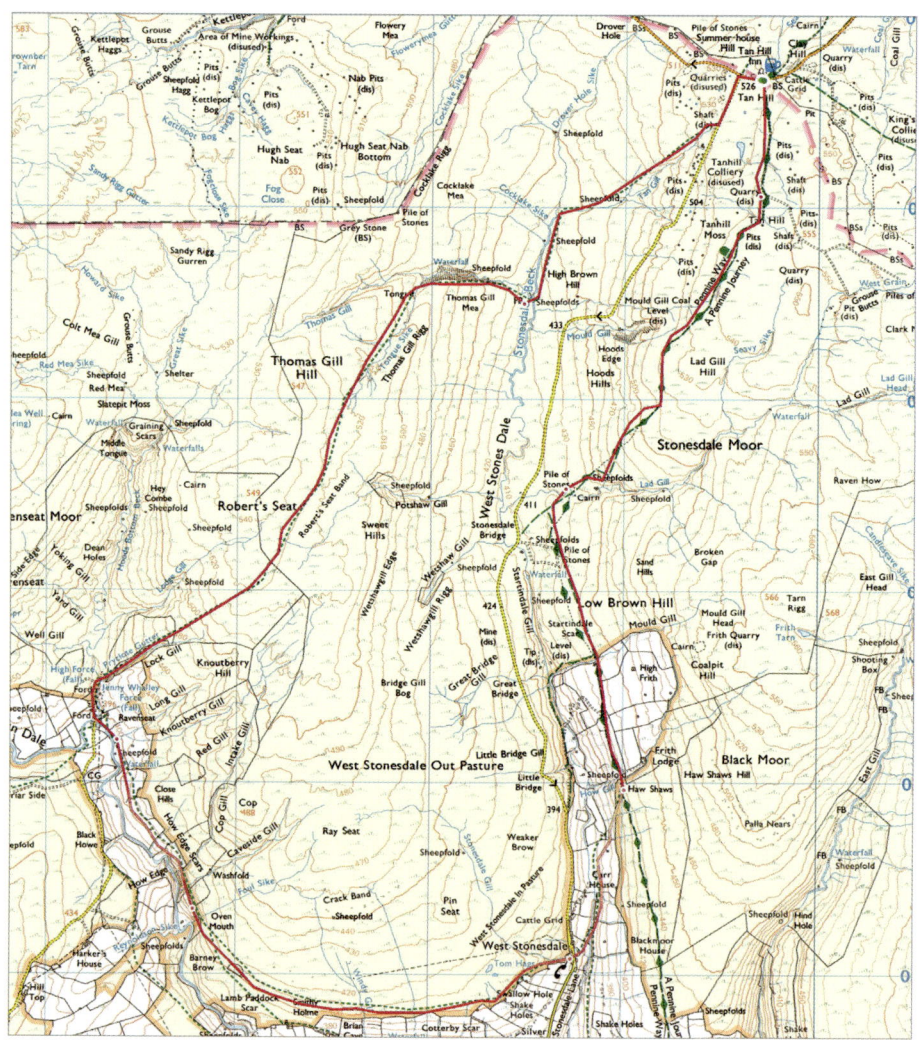

6

RIBBLEHEAD VIADUCT & THE STATION INN

— 7.2km (4.5 miles) —

The first thing that strikes you about the Ribblehead Viaduct is its sheer size. With 24 huge stone arches rising more than 30m (100ft) above the moors in North Yorkshire, it's a sight to behold. The viaduct is a scheduled monument, built between 1870 and 1874, and was at the time one of the most impressive engineering projects in England. It still carries the Settle–Carlisle railway line, which crosses the remote Yorkshire Dales and North Pennines. The route was saved in the 1980s by railway enthusiasts and the local community, and it has since grown in popularity to become one of the most famous scenic railway routes in the world. The 114km (71 miles) of track often plays host to both chartered and scheduled steam trains, the memorabilia of which is proudly on display in The Station Inn.

▲ The Station Inn sits down the road from the Ribblehead Train Station, on the famous Settle to Carlisle line.

There's a car park at The Station Inn, and it's worth wandering across the road to see the small, remote station at Ribblehead, just on the edge of the opening to the viaduct. It's indicative of a railway system in England that has long disappeared from mainstream life, the small platform and period buildings also housing a museum, which charts the history of the line.

THE WALK

From The Station Inn and its pub garden, you look down across the viaduct. To the right of the pub, there's a path that takes you across the eastern side of the bridge, its looming presence on your left and stretches of moorland in front of you. If you haven't found a parking space at the pub, there's a spacious parking area just down the hill at Sandy Hill, which often acts as the starting point of the walk.

Continue along the path with the viaduct on your left and views across the moorland and Runscar Hill on your right. At the first opportunity, as the viaduct curves elegantly around to the right, turn left towards Winterscales & Ivescar Farm. You'll pass under the bridge and along a track that winds around towards a collection of remote working farm buildings, home to around 130ha (320 acres) of upland grassland agriculture.

Continue on this track and you'll reach Ivescar, another collection of farm buildings, whose inhabitants seem to be made of stern stuff making a living treading on such unforgiving land. You'll have a choice here to turn left and cut the route short, or head on to Broadrake, at which point you turn left and cross Winterscales Beck, following the path until you reach a small road at a disused quarry.

Turn left here, with the beck to your right, and continue bearing right at each

▼ The Ribblehead Viaduct is one of England's greatest achievements of Victorian engineering.

opportunity as you return back towards the viaduct. Passing Gunnerfleet Farm, you'll then go under the viaduct again, though much nearer the road than on your outward-bound leg, and join the path back to the pub.

The Station Inn is an old-world celebration of the railway, decked out with the kind of carpet and red walls that wouldn't look out of place in a 1940s carriage owned by the illustrious 'Big Four' rail companies of the day. Misty-eyed paintings and photographs of the Settle–Carlisle Railway adorn the walls, but away from the nostalgia, there's a genuinely cosy atmosphere and a welcoming selection of local beers and food. Camper vans can park overnight in the pub car park, providing they use the facilities, and on a good weather day the real crowning glory is the fabulous garden, which offers unrivalled views across Batty Moss, the stretch of land the viaduct crosses.

> **THE PUB:** The Station Inn, Ribblehead, Low Sleights Rd, Carnforth, Lancs LA6 3AS
> www.thestationinnribblehead.com
> 01524 241274
>
> **START AND END POINT:** The Station Inn (see above)
>
> **WALK LENGTH:** 7.2km (4.5 miles)
>
> **ASCENT:** 100m (328ft)
>
> **APPROX. TIME:** 1 hour 45 minutes
>
> **PARKING:** At the junction of Gauber Rd, down the hill from The Station Inn
>
> **CAR FREE:** Ribblehead station for trains from Carlisle and Leeds, Station Inn bus stop for routes from Kirkby Lonsdale

The pub was built around the same time as the viaduct and it doubled as both a hostelry and a farm, providing shelter for the nearly 2,500 workers who built the viaduct, many of whom endured poor conditions, awful weather

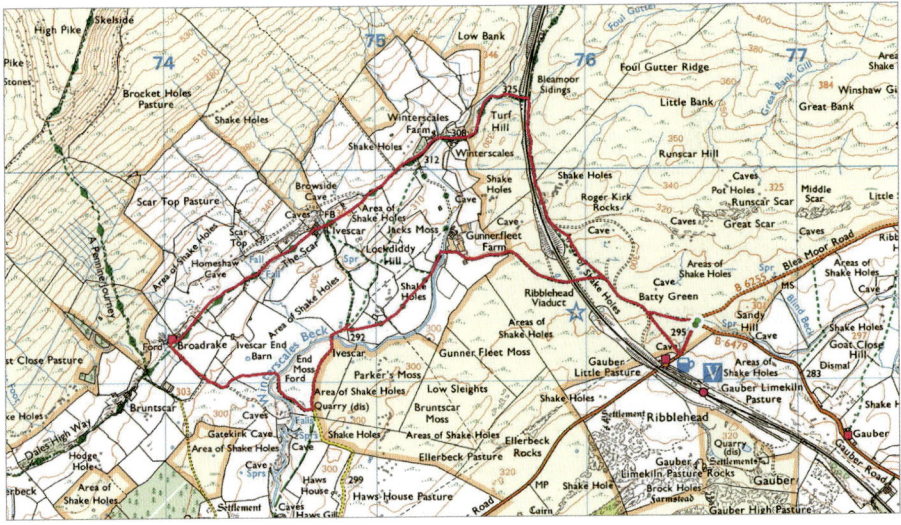

NORTH-WEST

and arduous manual labour. Over 100 men lost their lives during its creation. The railway line, and the bridge itself, was the last in England to be built using primarily manual labour, and there are photos from that era and various railway memorabilia to browse. The Station Inn attractively captures the essence of the rural north, and its rooms can also provide the base for a longer stay in the area.

◀ It's well worth arriving to this walk via the Ribblehead Station, on the Settle to Carlisle line.

▼ There's a welcoming feel to the pub, and you'd be forgiven for thinking you'd stepped into a period-correct railway carriage.

7

GREAT WHERNSIDE
& THE BLUE BELL INN

— 9.3km (5.8 miles) —

To many people, Kettlewell *is* the Yorkshire Dales. This small place encapsulates the essence of this part of the world and, situated in Upper Wharfedale, the surrounding landscape is a haven for outdoor enthusiasts, with some of the best walking and hiking trails in the area that cater to all levels of experience.

One such popular route is the ascent to Great Whernside, a prominent fell that provides panoramic views of the Dales. This family-friendly walk is not to be confused with the original Whernside, located near the Ribblehead Viaduct and the highest peak in the Dales. Rather, this walk is more diminutive but can still provide excellent views and is suitable for people of a range of different walking abilities. There are good waymarkers, excellent signage and plenty of walks on hard-standing surfaces.

It gets busy in Kettlewell through the summer seasons, but visit on an autumn or winter weekend and there are still little corners you'll have to yourself, particularly on this walk. There's an old-fashioned feeling here and the sleepy cottages and slow pace of life are complemented by the fresh, cleansing quality of the Kettlewell Beck, providing fresh water from high up on the dales.

▼ The lanes around the Dales here are a great example of Yorkshire at its most charming.

THE WALK

Park at the main, large car park at Kettlewell and cross the road into the heart of the village. Follow the road through the village, keeping the river on your left and passing the Kings Head pub. After around 180m (200 yards), past a handful of pretty terraced cottages, the road starts to turn into a stony path.

Continue on the stony path until you reach a choice of three different routes. For the most direct route, take the path signposted Providence Pot and Great Whernside via Hag Dyke (3.2km/2 miles), or if you want a slightly gentler initial climb, staying on the farm track toward Hay Tonge Farm is possible, before turning right to join the Hag Dyke path at the top. If you don't do this now, you can come back via this route.

Either way, once you're out of the village, closed farming fields soon make way to open fell land, with increasingly good views down towards Kettlewell and the valley below. It's well signed with regular fingerpost signs. The path becomes steeper as you reach Hag Dyke, an old, abandoned farmhouse that now serves as a Scout Hostel complete with its own little chapel, having been taken over by the Scouts in 1947. The hostel boasts solar and wind power and a large dining room, as well as heating in every room, which has no doubt been a welcome addition for hikers battling the elements over the decades.

Follow the footpath round the building and head up the steep section, which is rocky and can be uneven

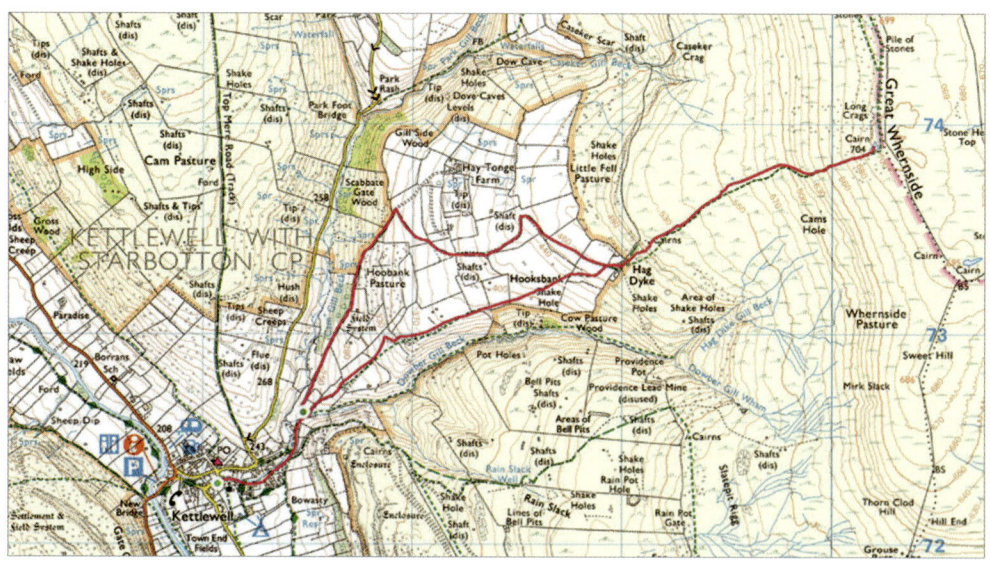

▼ Old mill buildings, since turned into places for locals to live, adorn the outskirts of the village of Kettlewell.

THE PUB: The Blue Bell Inn, Middle Ln, Kettlewell, Skipton, N. Yorks BD23 5QX
 www.bluebellkettlewell.com
 01756 760230

START AND END POINT: Kettlewell Car Park, Kettlewell, Skipton, N. Yorks BD23 5QZ

WALK LENGTH: 9.3km (5.8 miles)

ASCENT: 571m (1,873ft)

APPROX. TIME: 2 hours 45 minutes

PARKING: Kettlewell Car Park (see above)

CAR FREE: Kettlewell bus stop outside Bluebell Inn

you'll find a series of small stone steps that lead to the top. You're standing at 704m (2,310ft), marked by a cairn. On a clear day you'll be rewarded with panoramic views of the Dales, including Buckden Pike to the east and the Three Peaks of Pen-y-ghent, Ingleborough and Whernside to the west.

Heading back down, follow the boggy bit of the walk the same way you came up, and at the Hag Dyke hostel, take the other path (the one you didn't come up). If you've come up via the more direct route from Kettlewell, turn to the right through the gate and follow the rough access track away through the fields. Keep following this and soon you'll reach a junction with a gate. Turn left and follow the track all the way back down to Kettlewell. You can take the road back to the village and to the pub on your right, with its distinctive signage and bell hanging from the front façade.

underfoot – it's also boggier here as you head into wilder, open terrain populated by small streams that lead to larger rivers at a lower elevation. There are wonderful views around you, and although the path is ambiguous, it's easy to follow thanks to the thousands of feet before yours. At the summit,

▲ The Blue Bell Inn sits at the heart of the village of Kettlewell.

8

THE RIBBLE VALLEY & THE INN AT WHITEWELL

— 4km (2.5 miles) —

Deep in the heart of Lancashire lies the Ribble Valley. Expect to see plenty of bicycle riders here; the name has become synonymous with the Ribble Cycles company, one of the oldest bicycle manufacturers in the world and a leading innovator since the evolution of the modern bike in the late 19th century.

The area is burrowed within the broader expanse of the Lancashire countryside, and at the heart of the valley lies the River Ribble, which meanders through the landscape and lends its name to the area. The river's presence is a defining feature, shaping the valley's geography and contributing to its lush, verdant scenery. It's a far cry from its source at the Ribblehead Viaduct on the isolated moorland of the Yorkshire Dales – if you want to see where the river begins, there's also a walk in this book near here (see page 37).

At The Inn at Whitewell, you'll find a gentler scene. This former coaching house dates from the 16th century and is set above the River Hodder with rooms overlooking the sweeping expanse of countryside beyond. It's a large, imposing building and the hotel here is especially comfortable if you're staying a few days in the area. The jewel in its crown is 'The Piggeries', a converted set of farm buildings featuring three spacious double bedrooms in your own holiday house.

▼ Lush greenery, rolling hills and large farms take centre stage on this walk.

▼ Crossing the famous stepping stones over the river near the pub is a great way to start this walk.

THE WALK

Even if you're not staying, the expansive pub caters for all, and it's the starting point for this short walk, which can be squeezed into a lunchtime visit. Park in the car park and follow the signs for the stepping stones; these are charming steps that cross the river and head into open countryside beyond. Cross these, and head uphill towards the left until you reach a working farm called New Laund. After the farmyard, with tractors strewn around and relics of old agriculture charmingly visible, the view opens out to a large meadow with small buildings in the distance – this is Reed Barn Cottage.

Take the left-hand turn here instead of continuing along the field line and you'll gradually climb uphill, with excellent views off to your right, down to the valley and the hills beyond. New Laund Hill is to your left, and although there is no specific footpath up the hill, it's worth taking a short and steep stomp up, as the views are impressive. On the other side of the hill, you'll descend to a small farm track and a large expanse of grazing sheep. Go through the gate and emerge onto the little road.

Turn right on the road and start descending – the Ribble Valley Jubilee Trail meets the road here. Stay on the road and you'll walk past patches of woodland, with large farm buildings up bumpy tracks to your left. Continue

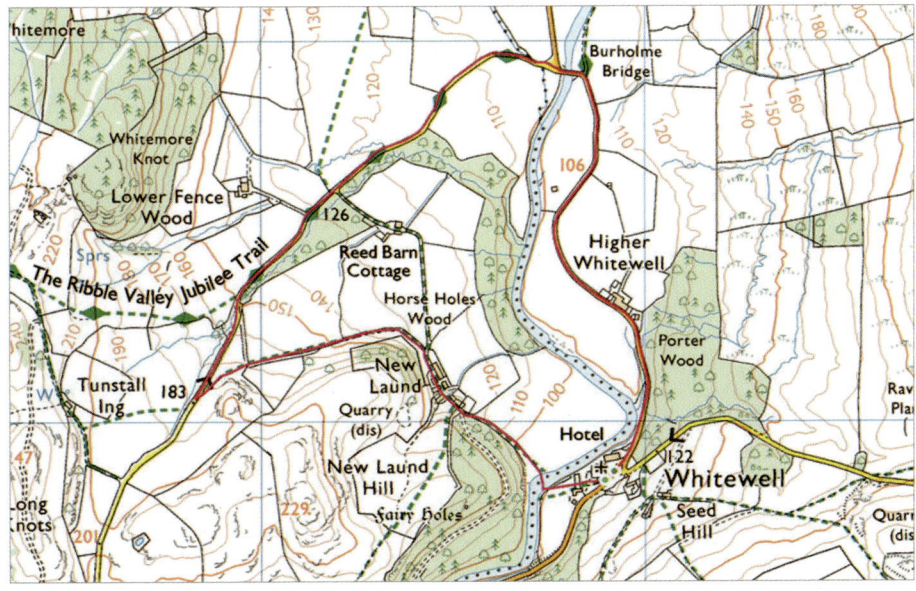

on the road and you'll reach a small 18th-century stone bridge across the River Hodder called Burholme Bridge – its two elliptical arches are instantly recognisable. Go over the bridge, turn right onto the larger road and walk along this for a short distance – be careful, as this is an often-used road by locals.

Before long, you'll reach a signpost on your right, which allows you access to a permissive path across neighbouring farmland. Take this, turn left and walk across the fields with the hedgerows on your left. Before long, The Inn at Whitewell looms into view and you'll rejoin the river at the edge of Porter Wood. Go into the woodland, over a small bridge and back to the pub.

In addition to the large bar areas at the pub, there's also a generous terrace overlooking the countryside you've just walked through, as well as a lovely local bookshop inside and all the amenities you'd expect from a well-appointed hotel. If you have extra time, ask at the bar for a walking guide as the pub produces a good selection of routes themselves, which offer a variety of

▲ Inside The Inn at Whitewell, you'll find a cosy dining and bar area.

▼ The Burholme Bridge is a local landmark spanning the River Hodder.

hikes in the Ribble Valley. Be sure to ask about the weird and wonderful – the Ribble Valley is steeped in myth and legend. Further south, at the Hodder Bridge near Stonyhurst, there is said to be the ghost of a monk who drowned in the river. Local legend says his figure can sometimes be seen walking the bridge at night. Also be sure to look out for the Tolkien Trail and follow the famous 'Middle Earth' walk through the countryside that inspired the writer.

THE PUB: The Inn at Whitewell, Forest of Bowland, Clitheroe, Lancs BB7 3AT
 www.innatwhitewell.com
 01200 448222

START AND END POINT: The Inn at Whitewell (see above)

WALK LENGTH: 4km (2.5 miles)

ASCENT: 104m (341ft)

APPROX. TIME: 1 hour 20 minutes

PARKING: Outside the Inn at Whitewell (see above)

CAR FREE: The Inn at Whitewell to/from Settle Market Place

▼ During the summer seasons, the farmland around this area is awash with wildflowers.

9

HEBDEN BRIDGE & PACK HORSE INN

— 12.2km (7.6 miles) —

The fast-flowing rivers and streams around the area of Hebden Bridge were once the driving force behind large-scale English industrialisation. Here, the River Calder and Hebden Water meet, carved out of deep valleys and lush wooded areas that rise steeply thanks to the Pennine hills that emerge on either side of the Calder Valley.

This water originally powered mills and workshops, and the area grew rapidly during the 19th century when it became a hub for the textile industry, particularly in cotton and wool production. The population has grown around the wool trade since the medieval period and the town's narrow, cobbled streets and historic buildings still reflect a multitude of different eras, with workman's cottages, warehouses and 'double-decker' buildings that were built to suit the town's steep, narrow valley sides.

Further out of town, the moorland and countryside around Hebden Bridge show the scars of industry, too. It's remote here, isolated and windswept, and this is a decent walk in length that takes in the National Trust-managed Hardcastle Crags wooded area, before emerging high up onto the moorland by the Pack Horse Inn, with fantastic views across this old industrial landscape.

THE WALK

It's easiest to park at Midgehole Car Park, which is owned by the National Trust. Here, you'll be greeted by a series of waymarked paths; the easiest thing to do is stroll upstream with the flowing waters on your right. The path is densely wooded – almost hidden – but it's a joy to walk next to the path that crashes around weirs, over boulders and through rapids up to Gibson Mill. This is one of the National Trust's flagship eco projects and it houses a café as well as exhibition spaces. It has been off-grid for more than 10 years and all its energy is generated onsite – natural springs in the woodland also provide the water supply.

Once you're past Gibson Mill, continue through the woodland to its most northern edge, and you'll emerge onto a high lane. Turn west on a small lane that dips down, crosses the beck on a bridge and rises up the other side towards Blakedean Scout Hostel and the Pack Horse Inn.

This 17th-century inn has long been a welcoming stop for travellers, its name harking back to the inn's origins as a

▼ Gibson Mill sits at the heart of the National Trust managed Hardcastle Crags, a lovely wooded area for family-friendly walking.

THE PUB: Pack Horse Inn, Widdop Rd, Hebden Bridge, W. Yorks HX7 7AT
🌐 www.thepackhorseinn.co.uk
📞 01422 844614

START AND END POINT: Midgehole Car Park (National Trust), Midgehole Rd, Hebden Bridge, W. Yorks HX7 7AL

WALK LENGTH: 12.2km (7.6 miles)

ASCENT: 388m (1,273ft)

APPROX. TIME: 3 hours 10 minutes

PARKING: Midgehole Car Park (see above)

CAR FREE: Hardcastle Crags bus stop (request stop) near the car park

resting place for packhorse trains, which were essential to the transport of goods across the challenging terrain of the Pennines. These packhorses would carry wool, cloth and other goods between Yorkshire and Lancashire, traversing the old trails that crisscrossed the moorlands. The inn provided food, drink and shelter for both the drovers and their animals, becoming a crucial waypoint.

When you're ready to leave, cross the road and take the path north, directly outside the pub, towards Walshaw Dean Lower Reservoir, turning right at Holme Ends and crossing a small

▲ Hardcastle Crags is a spectacular wooded valley of more than 160ha (400 acres).

▶ Many of the routes above the wooded valley used to act as packhorse trails, for moving cloth and wool across this rural terrain.

NORTH-WEST

bridge over Alcomden Water. From here you can continue along the well-marked farm track east towards Walshaw, with expansive views across to the moorland on your right.

From Walshaw, follow Cow Hey Lane, a rough track that offers not only fantastic views but a great insight into life in this part of the world – sheep border the track, old working farmers go about their daily lives and patched-up Land Rovers sweep over the rural terrain in the same way they've done thousands of times before. When you reach the tiny farming hamlet of Shackleton, you'll see a gate on your right, opposite a farmhouse – follow the footpath sign, which will lead you back down to the woodland and eventually to your car at Midgehole Car Park.

10

SANDSTONE TRAIL & THE PHEASANT INN

— 6.4km (4 miles) —

The Sandstone Trail stretches over 55km (34 miles) through the counties of Cheshire and Shropshire. Established in 1974, the trail offers a diverse range of landscapes, with a mixture of rocky outcrops, lush woodlands and large open farmland to explore.

The dramatic sandstone ridges that give the trail its name were formed over 200 million years ago, and provide a rich diversity of habitats for local wildlife and plant life. During the warmer months, the soil here provides the perfect environment for wildflowers and much of its protected landscapes also offer safe havens for butterflies, moths, dragonflies and a mixture of avian life. During this relatively short walk through a section of the Sandstone Trail, there's the opportunity to experience a mixture of the types of landscape typical of this area, and The Pheasant Inn also makes a great stopping-off point for people interested in doing the whole trail.

THE WALK

From the pub car park, go out onto the small lane and walk downhill, keeping to the left, and then turning left when the road splits. You'll then bend back round on yourself and keep right at the fork, passing a small cottage. If you look right, about 90m (100 yards) down this lane, you'll see the Sandstone Trail emerging from the hedgerow on your right. This is where you'll return from at the end of the walk.

For now, keep going straight, passing some farm buildings on the right-hand side and then a gate, which forms the boundary to the Peckforton Hills. As you enter the forestry area, take a moment to breathe in the smell of the trees around you and enjoy the sheer scale of them; there are hundreds of trees here that tower above you, so during quiet days on the trail it feels a little bit like having a slice of enchanted forest all to yourself.

Keep on this path and it'll begin to narrow at the same time as dropping slightly downhill and bending round to the left. You'll see the remains of an old bridge, which carries a disused railway track that would have once served the local quarries. Immediately past this bridge, a stile on the right climbs into a large adjacent field, with the views opening up majestically to the flat farmland below and, in the distance, the hazy hills of the Peak District.

There's an obvious path to follow across this field that has been used for centuries, keeping the forest and field boundary on your right. Originally called Baws Lane, the path ran down to Stonehouse Farm, and that's exactly where this walk goes until you reach a couple of stiles that take you onto Stone House Lane. Turn right here.

Partly thanks to the amount of land available to farm across the Cheshire Plains, the farms here are large, capacious houses and their outbuildings pepper this lane, hidden behind rambly cottage gardens and appearing grand in an unassuming, unpretentious way. The walk now continues on Stone House Lane for about 500m (550 yards) before you see a small layby on the side of the road, the

> **THE PUB:** The Pheasant Inn, Higher Burwardsley, Tattenhall, Ches CH3 9PF
> 🌐 www.thepheasantinn.co.uk
> ☎ 01829 770434
>
> **START AND END POINT:** The Pheasant Inn (see above)
>
> **WALK LENGTH:** 6.4km (4 miles)
>
> **ASCENT:** 181m (594ft)
>
> **APPROX. TIME:** 1 hour 30 minutes
>
> **PARKING:** Car park at The Pheasant Inn (see above)
>
> **CAR FREE:** Bus stop on Stone House Lane in Peckforton for buses to/from Nantwich

▼ Large, flat farmland dominates the landscape here, with hints of the hills of the Peak District beyond.

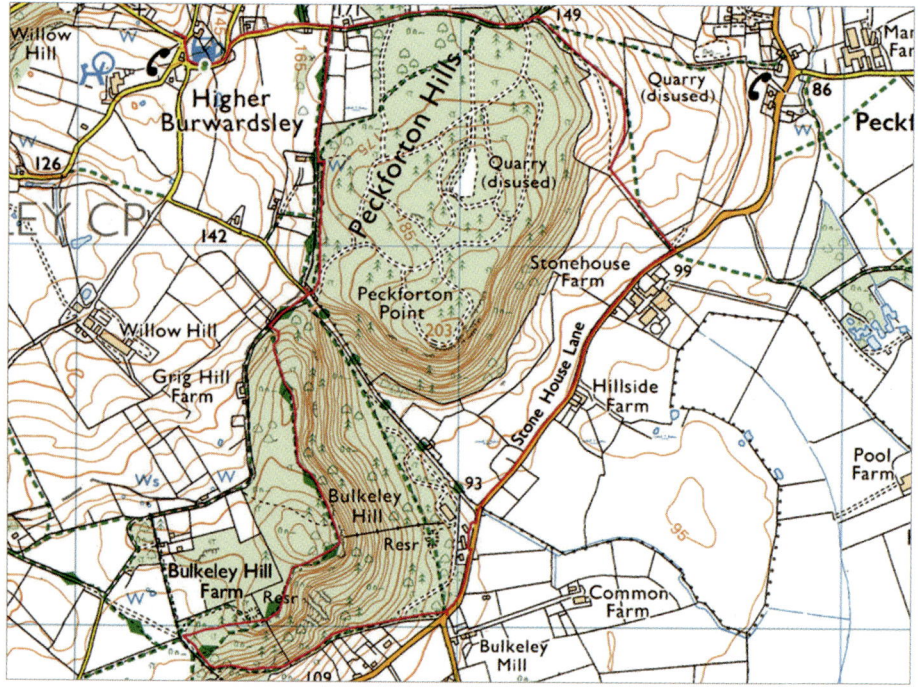

entrance to Bulkeley Hill and a wooden trail next to a National Trust sign.

This southern area of the Peckforton Hill Range is managed by the Trust and is a semi-natural ancient woodland of just over 32ha (80 acres) that sits on sandstone bedrock. Take the trail to the left, and you'll find yourself weaving uphill through a maze of twisted and knurled trees – much of this deadwood is kept to help preserve habitats and the abundant array of wildlife found here. This is a Site of Special Scientific Interest (SSSI) thanks to its habitats and its lowland health, which is rare in this part of the world. When you reach a crossroads with several paths converging, take the right-hand path and continue uphill through larger, more open spaces that lead to the summit of Bulkeley Hill.

When it's time to catch your breath at the top, you're rewarded with views across the Peaks and surrounding farms, including the pretty village of Peckforton. Look south and you'll see the earthworks of an Iron Age hill fort, which is still remarkably well preserved despite all the quarrying and mining that's taken place across the last few centuries.

Here the Sandstone Trail follows the top of the ridge, and on clear days there are excellent views through the swaying trees. It's a quiet place, high above the villages and the noise of the main roads that link Stoke-on-Trent to Chester and Wrexham. Don't turn off this path – when you start going downhill and see a large building with big gates at the front, turn left and then immediately right to follow the Sandstone Trail signs.

It's a straight run on this path back to where you started, and you'll pass a handful of smallholdings on your left, with animals cheerily running free, and emerging orchards that hint at a prosperous rural homespun economy. Once you reach the road, turn left and follow it back down, retracing your steps back to the pub.

The Pheasant Inn would have been a farm originally, but there are records showing that in the 1650s there were three ale houses in the village of Burwardsley, and this establishment was almost certainly one of them. There have been additions and alterations over the years, and today the main pub has a superb dining hall area, with stable and barn outbuildings that have been converted into rooms to stay. Today, it's well-appointed and well-connected, but the rural setting meant that there was no running water here until 1936, and no electricity until the late 1940s. The pub has a great selection of CAMRA-approved local ales and the menu is elevated British fair, most of the ingredients of which come from the immediate vicinity. I speak from experience – their signature cocktails are best enjoyed by the roaring fire on a cosy autumn day.

▲ The hearth at the heart of the bar area in The Pheasant, provides a welcome resting spot for hikers in the nearby hills.

▼ The Pheasant Inn sits nestled within a small collection of buildings in the Peckforton Hills.

NORTH-EAST

From the coal mines to the famous shipyards, the north-east of England bears the weight of its industrial history. At the same time, it's a region of stunning remoteness and isolation, being one of the least populated areas in the country. Here, walkers can explore a blend of sharp cliffs, sweeping beaches and old fishing villages that cling to the coastline. The wind-whipped shores of places like Bamburgh (see page 64), perched on the edge of the North Sea, are some of the quietest and most beautiful beaches anywhere in England. These coastal areas have long been both a source of sustenance and a line of defence, with castles standing high above the water, protecting against centuries of invasion.

Inland, the landscape transforms into the rolling countryside of Northumberland and County Durham. Wide hills give way to the open expanses of the North Pennines and the wild, lonely beauty of the Cheviot Hills. Marked by ancient stone walls and scattered farms, these areas tell the story of a land dominated by sheep farming and agricultural life. The Northumberland National Park (see pages 76 and 80), with its heather-clad moors and hidden valleys, feels untouched by time. Some of the most remote and unspoilt walks in this book can be found here. Further south, the North York Moors (see pages 89 and 93) offer similarly stunning walks, with sweeping vistas towards the coastline and nearby towns and cities.

As a frontier region, the north-east has long been shaped by the comings and goings of people from across Europe. During the Viking Age, Norsemen were drawn by the wealth of monasteries and the strategic importance

of the area's rivers, launching repeated raids that left a lasting imprint on the land. The medieval period saw the rise of powerful castles and fortresses, with cities like Newcastle, Durham and Alnwick becoming centres of political and military power. Durham Cathedral, one of the great masterpieces of Norman architecture, still dominates the skyline.

More latterly, the coalfields of County Durham and Northumberland fuelled the factories, railways and steamships that powered the country's rise to global prominence. Beneath the land's surface, generations of miners extracted the 'black gold' that would fuel the engines of the empire. Entire communities sprang up around the collieries in villages of terraced houses where families lived, worked and often died, in the shadow of the pithead. Mining was more than a job, it was a way of life, with its own traditions, dialect and social bonds, and many of the walks featured in this region commemorate this legacy.

Shipbuilding, too, was central to the region's economy, particularly in the cities. The River Tyne became synonymous with the construction of mighty vessels, from merchant ships to warships that helped shape the fortunes of this land. While the decline of coal mining and shipbuilding brought challenges, the north-east has since embraced regeneration. New industries like renewable energy and digital technology are beginning to take root, offering a sense of hope and renewal. Today, wind farms and green energy initiatives are leading the way toward a more sustainable future, set against the backdrop of this quiet, remote and unspoilt landscape.

11

HOLY ISLAND CIRCULAR & THE SHIP INN

— 5.6km (3.5 miles) —

There is a reason why wandering over to the shores of Lindisfarne, otherwise known as Holy Island, feels like an otherworldly experience. This flat landscape can feel like a different planet, and separated from the rest of Northumberland twice a day by the tide, it has an atmosphere all of its own. Its landscape and story played a huge part in the history of how England became the place we know today. Timing your visit right is key, as high tide blocks off all access to Holy Island, and the water rises quickly. It doesn't need to be written into the pages of this book what fate has befallen the vehicles of those drivers who have misjudged the clock, or not heeded the ominous warning signs at either end of the causeway, but provided you have a tide table to hand this is an easy day out and an opportunity to go through a portal into an alternative world.

The Lindisfarne National Nature Reserve, which contains the muddy, flat land you cross as you drive over the causeway as well as much of the surrounding salt marshes and dunes, dominates the landscape around here, and this walk offers wildlife watchers the chance to spot some of Britain's most sought-after fauna. Geese from the northern reaches of the Arctic Circle, waders, wildfowl and large numbers of grey seals all call this island home, and the options of circular walks around the island provide great opportunities to get up close to these animals.

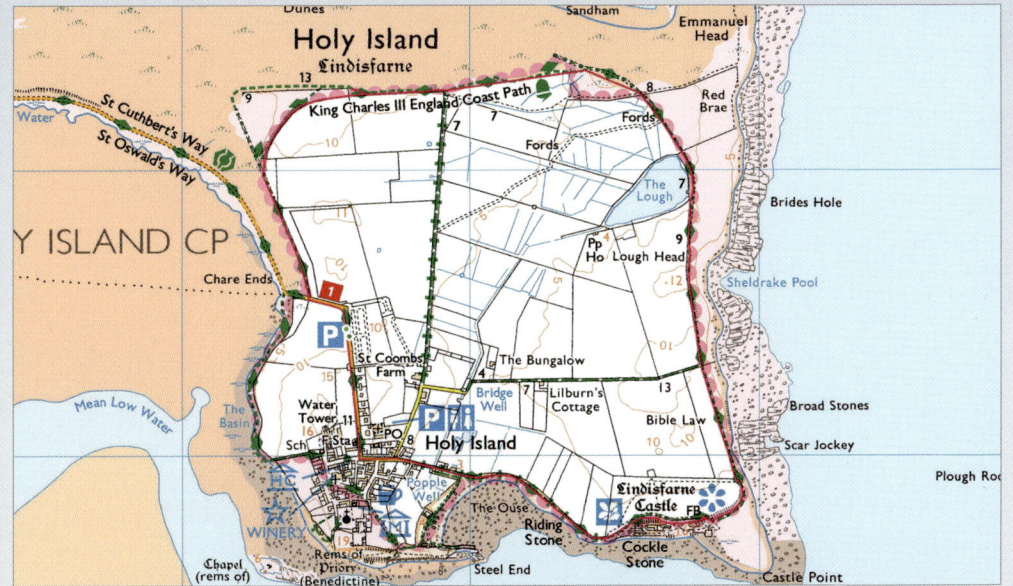

When it comes to the human-made part of this world, the castle and world-famous priory, which was the last physical manifestation of the beginning of Christian teachings in England, dominate the landscape. Ransacked by Vikings in the 8th century as part of a series of raids on the Northumbrian coastline, the priory's inhabitants were killed or kidnapped and it wasn't until the arrival of St Cuthbert in the late 10th century that it was revived. The stone relics you see today date back to the Normans' arrival in the 11th century.

THE WALK

At Holy Island Chare Ends Car Park, instead of heading to the priory or the castle, like many people tend to do, this walk starts by going in the opposite direction, towards the north of the island and the sand dunes known as The Links. It's not long before you reach a sandy, bleak landscape that's at the mercy of chilly Scandinavian winds – be sure to wrap up warm. Bear round to the right

▼ Holy Island is an enchanting landscape, and one many wildlife call home while on their migration journeys.

THE PUB: The Ship Inn, Holy Island, Berwick-upon-Tweed, Northumb TD15 2SJ
🌐 www.theshipinn-holyisland.co.uk
📞 01289 389311

START AND END POINT: Holy Island Chare Ends Car Park, Berwick-upon-Tweed, Northumb TD15 2SE

WALK LENGTH: 5.6km (3.5 miles)

ASCENT: 27m (89ft)

APPROX. TIME: 1 hour 20 minutes

PARKING: Holy Island Chare Ends Car Park (see above)

CAR FREE: Chare Ends bus stop on Holy Island for services from Berwick Railway Station

and continue on, following the obvious line and keeping the fence on your right.

Before long, you'll come across a turning to Emmanuel Head, a great white structure built by Trinity House in the early 19th century to act as a daymark and provide navigation guidance to passing ships. It's thought that it could actually be England's oldest daymark, and at 10.7m (35ft) high, it's an imposing structure. To the left of this there's a small path that leads to a charming, diminutive sandy beach called Sandham Bay.

Back the way you came, and Lindisfarne Castle looms into view, rising imposingly from a rocky outcrop on the southern end of the island. Pass a small lough (lake) on the right of the footpath, and it's at this point that you'll start to see more visitors as you get closer to the attractions that bring millions of people here every year. You can pass the castle on the footpath that surrounds the outcrop, but while you're here it's worth paying a visit to the Victorian lime kilns down by the sea. They're some of the best-preserved kilns in the country and were once used to make the quicklime used as render for buildings in the area, and other domestic items like disinfectant and soap. You can see why the industry was a dangerous one if you consider the heat involved amid the enormous furnaces you now stand in.

Within the town at Holy Island, you'll soon come across a small fishing harbour. Not far past that, in the area known as Marygate and nearly back to where you started, step inside The Ship Inn. Known as 'The Tavern' by villagers and locals, there's been a pub here for as long as anyone can remember, and should you wish to immerse yourself in the ghostly spirituality of Lindisfarne Priory, there are four rooms you can stay in, bookable in advance. This is a family-run free house and now even has its own distillery, where the sought-after Holy Island Gin

▲ Follow in the footsteps of ancient monks who built Lindisfarne Priory, nearly 1,400 years ago.

NORTH-EAST
62

▲ Holy Island has a captivating history of maritime adventure and industry. Much of this is documented on the walls of the pub.

is manufactured. It has a faintly old-fashioned and charming wood-panelled bar, with a generous beer garden outside for sunnier days. Life at sea is never far away, and it's also worth spending some time looking at the various photographs and paintings that portray a history of island life, from days past to the present-day vibrant community that calls this distinctive, spiritual place home.

▼ Strolling along the dune-lined paths on Holy Island is a great way to see the wildlife and sights that make this such a unique location for a walk.

12

SEAHOUSES TO BAMBURGH CIRCULAR & THE OLDE SHIP INN

— 12.7km (7.9 miles) —

There is what feels like an old-fashioned seaside charm to Seahouses, the middle town in a chain of three distinctive communities – Beadnell to the south, and Bamburgh to the north. What links the three of them is a truly captivating stretch of coastline. With the looming, often foreboding North Sea stretched out ahead of you, the wind whistles and the cold air has a sharper touch in this part of the world. The town's harbour, framed by the largest hotel in the area and its adjoining lifeboat station, is where boats shelter from the storm. It has the air of a real sanctuary, conjuring up the atmosphere of a rich and dramatic maritime history.

This was once a thriving port named 'North Sunderland', which that developed as a strategic trading centre thanks to its advantageous location along the North Sea coast. The herring industry initially brought prosperity to the town, with merchants lining the streets to export fish to other seaside towns and buying coal, lime, salt and various agricultural products for the rest of Northumberland from boats plying their trade up and down the coastline. The town also played a major part in the two World Wars, and as a gateway to such a strategically important piece of sea, military fortifications were installed in the town and the harbour served as a base for minesweepers.

▼ As a privately owned residence, Bamburgh Castle is one of the largest inhabited castles in the country.

THE WALK

Looking out towards the harbour, with the boats on your right, this walk takes you further north to the village of Bamburgh and its impressive castle, which stands as a fortification against invaders from the east. There was a Celtic Briton hill fort at this location before the Roman conquest, and in the late 8th and 9th centuries, Vikings invaded. The castle changed hands several times, playing an important role in the Wars of the Roses, eventually falling into disrepair after the English Civil War. Now, it's a popular tourist destination in private hands, with many events taking place across the year.

From Seahouses, continue north past the harbour, keeping the sea on your right, until you reach St Aidan's Dunes and Monks House Rocks – on a clear day, you should see the Farne Islands on the right. The Monks House, still a small hamlet on these windswept islands, was originally a collection of buildings on a patch of land gifted by Henry II in the 13th century to the islands' monks so they could build a granary and storehouse.

Past Greenhill Rocks, you'll now walk along the beach. A huge, expansive and wild place with miles of golden sands, flanked by pristine dunes. The wind often comes straight in here, which makes it a great spot for kiteboarding

THE PUB: The Olde Ship Inn, Main St, Seahouses, Northumb NE68 7RD
🌐 www.theoldeship.co.uk
📞 01665 720200

START AND END POINT: The Olde Ship Inn (see above)

WALK LENGTH: 12.7km (7.9 miles)

ASCENT: 76m (249ft)

APPROX. TIME: 3 hours

PARKING: Seafield Car Park, Seahouses, Northumb NE68 7RQ

CAR FREE: King Street bus stop in Seahouses, from Berwick and Alnwick

and windsurfing. Round the corner of the beach, and the impressive sight of Bamburgh Castle looms into view – keep going for 1.6km (1 mile) or so and there's an easy scramble across the dunes to Links Road and the castle's car park. Continue, and you'll find the ramp up to the castle's entrance.

Although the castle is the undisputed jewel of the area, rising dramatically from its volcanic outcrop above the village, there are other sights to enjoy here. It's worth visiting the Grace Darling Museum, which charts the crucial role this local heroine played in a daring sea rescue in 1838

that set up the precedent for the RNLI as we know it today.

Walk through the village to journey back to Seahouses, continuing on to the Victoria Hotel and from there, turning left onto Ingram Road. This road becomes more and more rural as you walk, with low walls to your left and sheep fields stretching down to the sea, with an excellent view behind you of the castle.

Halfway down this lane, after a right turn towards East Burton, turn left back towards the sea with a defensive bunker in front of you. Walk past this and join a lane at Saddlers Hall, then follow this rough track towards a collection of houses at Shoreston Hall. At the T-junction, the path crosses the road (look slightly right and follow the fingerpost sign), and continues along fields towards the outskirts of Seahouses. Follow the sign to North Sunderland and you'll emerge over a stile onto Broad Road. Turn left here, and then right once you meet Main Street, and follow the road back to the harbour and The Olde Ship Inn.

Once through the door of the pub, you'll be greeted by a huge array of Northumberland nautical memorabilia, from knots and ropes to navigation equipment and models of local fishing vessels that adorn every wall, nook and

▲ Locals enjoying a pint among the nautical items on display in the pub.

cranny of the pub. A roaring fire keeps the cold North Sea wind away.

The pub has been in the same family ownership since 1910, and the public bar has been altered very little since the pub's opening in 1745. Although tourists are prevalent at any time of day or night, there's no doubt that there will be a few local Northumbrians propping up the bar, recounting their tales of living on the edge of England. The backdrop of nautical life is spectacular in both its quantity and diversity, and you won't find it hard to imagine similar stories being told in the thrashing gales of yesteryear by generations of people who know this land and these seas better than anyone.

▼ Seahouses Harbour is a haven for small fishing vessels and pleasure boats.

◄ The vast expanse of the beach at Bamburgh is best enjoyed in the quiet seasons, when you'll often have huge stretches to yourself.

NORTH-EAST

13

CRASTER, DUNSTANBURGH CASTLE, LOW NEWTON-BY-THE-SEA & THE SHIP INN

— 12.4km (7.7 miles) —

'I must go down to the seas again,' writes John Masefield, and there are few places in the north-east of England where you are more aptly able to answer the call of the running tide than along the coast path north from the small fishing village of Craster up to the beautifully formed Newton-by-the-Sea.

Craster conjures the senses. From the sound of the rhythmic pull of the tide echoing through the village to the smell of traditional oak-smoked kippers, little has changed here in centuries. Craster's smokehouses, where this age-old smoking process still takes place to this day, stand as guardians to a unique culinary tradition in this area, and continue a practice that has defined the village for generations. The fishing heritage here is palpable; weathered nets and lobster pots line the harbour, a testament to the village's reliance on the bounty of the North Sea.

▲ Dunstanburgh Castle on the horizon with a view down to Low Newton.

THE WALK

From the heart of the village of Craster, look north and the majestic ruins of Dunstanburgh Castle are obvious, with the winding coast path stretching beyond the immediate shelter of the village. This medieval fortress, perched atop a windswept headland, is a tangible link to Northumberland's past, and as you head north on the coast path towards the castle the smell of smoking kippers gradually disappears behind you.

The crashing sea takes centre stage on your right, and when the weather is good this feels like a benign stretch of path. But during the winter storms, it would pay to be wary of the waves. In the low seasons you'll benefit from some breathtakingly empty stretches of beach in Northumberland, and it's one of my favourite places to visit in the winter.

After just 1.6km (1 mile) on this stretch of path you'll reach the castle. The Great Whin Sill, a stretch of rock that passes from the Pennines to the Northumbrian coast, finally breaks ground here and forms the base of the outcrop on which the castle stands atop. It's an impressive sight, and you can either choose to visit the castle or follow the path round to the left on its inland side.

◀ The Ship Inn and its small village green, provide a perfect resting spot while at the beach. Fringed by pretty fishing cottages.

▲ Inside The Ship Inn there's a rustic, well-laid out dining space.

here, walking beside the sea and soaking up the calm, almost untouched feel. Compared to some of the other places on the coastline in the north-east, this feels subdued, family-friendly and well set up for lazy summer days spent with a windbreak and a cricket set.

At the far end of the beach, and near the point at which the walk doubles back on itself, you come to Low Newton. Here, it pays to look back on where you've come from, as the view back towards the castle is most striking, the sandy bay perfectly framing its looming shadow on the horizon. The view is especially impressive during sunrise or sunset, when the castle's silhouette is beautifully highlighted.

There's a holiday atmosphere in Low Newton. As you approach this diminutive village, you'll see a square of tiny fishing cottages on three sides and a village green in the middle, which provides the perfect space to sit and watch the waves with a pint from the pub. There's a mix of local

Embleton Bay then stretches out in front of you, its beach a sweeping crescent of windswept sand fringed by sand dunes, and beyond that the manicured landscape of Dunstanburgh Castle Golf Course. Continue along

▶ A delightful summer scene at Low Newton-by-the-Sea.

accommodation and holiday rentals here, and it's easy to imagine the fishing community of days gone by gathering to share stories of their catches, repair nets and pass the time, sheltered by the cottages from the whistling North Sea wind. Much of the land around Low Newton-by-the-Sea is owned and managed by the National Trust, which ensures the preservation of the area, but a glance at the noticeboard in The Ship Inn reveals an active year-round community. The village hosts various events throughout the year, from traditional cèilidh dances to fêtes and village fairs.

THE PUB: The Ship Inn, Low Newton, Northumb NE66 3EL
www.shipinnnewton.co.uk
01665 576262

START AND END POINT: Craster Harbour, Alnwick, Northumb NE66 3TR

WALK LENGTH: 12.4km (7.7 miles) (Low Newton from Craster and back again)

ASCENT: 99m (325ft)

APPROX. TIME: 2 hours 45 minutes

PARKING: Craster Quarry Car Park, W End Craster, Northumb NE66 3TS

CAR FREE: Craster Harbour bus stop for routes from Berwick and Alnwick

14

ALWIN RIVER & THE ROSE AND THISTLE

— 7km (4.4 miles) —

The village of Alwinton must be in one of the prettiest positions in the Northumberland countryside. There's a simple, unspoilt beauty here, and the village itself has a quiet agricultural atmosphere, the barks of hundreds of generations of sheepdogs echoing around the hills that surround this evocative valley. The area radiates the feeling of stepping in the footsteps of previous generations; this walk takes us on drove roads and hidden tracks between borders that contribute to much of the rural history in this area.

As you drive into Alwinton, look across the valley to the hills that surround the village, and then at the small cluster of houses and farm buildings that form the village. If there's wood smoke rising, it's likely coming from The Rose and Thistle pub, a small, old-fashioned watering hole that forms the start and end point of this walk. The pub itself is a cosy spot to shelter from the often misty, changeable weather around here, and it's also a haven for the farmers and members of the local community who work this land all year round.

THE WALK

With the front door of The Rose and Thistle pub on your right, you'll be facing a small village green, with benches around its perimeter and views to the fields beyond. Cross the green and join a very small track signposted Border Ridge. Continue on until you reach a ladder stile, at which point the track skirts around a former Iron Age settlement. There will be a point slightly further down this track that the lane itself bears round to the left – you'll be going right here, passing a gate and following the path across fields that now start to lead gently uphill and to the highest point on the walk, with lovely views down to the River Alwin.

At this point, you'll be looking across ancient pathways. Clennell Street, as the track you've come from is called, is an important centuries-old trading route between this area of northern England and Scotland, and Alwinton is

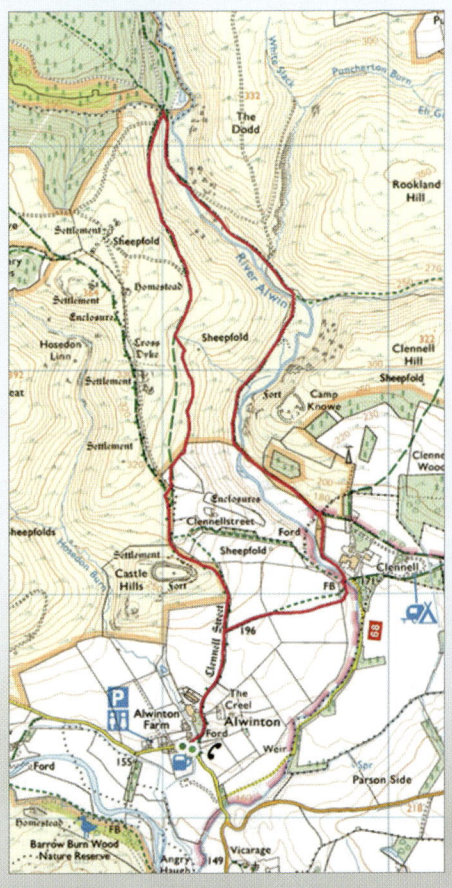

▼ The walks around these hills are on ancient tracks, often used as trading routes between England and Scotland.

a popular starting spot for the Border Ridge walk that can also be undertaken on horseback or mountain bike. Drovers, shepherds and traders used this route, plying their goods backwards and forward across remote, wild and windswept borders that were and arguably still are impossible to police or monitor – these are far-off lands. Farms on the hill here were used as stopping-off points for smugglers, who were selling their wares and hiding from the prying eyes of wandering excise men.

If you continue on this path, you'll be heading downhill to a corner of Kidland Forest, bearing back on yourself to follow the charming route of the River Alwin. You'll cross the river a few times here, with the quiet babbling of the water soundtracking your walk and, at the right time of year, wildflowers and long grass meadows bordering the river. You'll reach a crossroads at the end of this river walk, and on the fringes of Clennell Hall, follow the track round to the right to get across the fields and back to Clennell Street. Turn left and follow the path back the way you came up to return to Alwinton and the pub.

There's little to distinguish The Rose and Thistle from any of the small farm buildings or terraced cottages that line the lanes in the village. Through the door, however, there's the familiar quiet and warmth of a pub set up to be a refuge for anyone at any time of day or night, year-round, no matter the weather. Posters line the walls, marking the history and heritage of the famous sheepdog trials, agricultural shows and competitions that take place in the area. There are comfortable chairs and sofas spread across the large main room that have seated generations of storytellers. The warm glow of the fire fills the room, and in good weather, there's also the opportunity to open large doors and eat in the garden, with views across to the West Wood and the Ramshaugh plantation beyond.

It's the perfect quiet spot to dry off over a pint, watching the mist roll across the tops of the trees on the hills beyond,

◀ There's little to mark the Rose and Thistle out from the other buildings in the area, but you can be sure of a warm welcome inside.

NORTH-EAST

and it's likely you'll be joined by other walkers descending into the valley and leaving their muddy boots at the door. If you're staying for longer, there's also the opportunity to eat a classic pub menu and stay in the B&B rooms, which will soon be having an upgrade. Time it right, and you'll also get to experience the pub's unique position at the centre of Alwinton life: hosting events to support the Alwinton Border Shepherds' Show, one of the largest traditional country sheepdog trials in the area, with local produce on display and activities such as wrestling and fell running bringing in a large audience each year.

THE PUB: The Rose and Thistle, Alwinton, Morpeth, Northumb NE65 7BQ
www.facebook.com/roseandthistlealwinton
01669 650226

START AND END POINT: Alwinton Car Park, 1 Gallow Law, Alwinton, Morpeth, Northumb NE65 7BQ

WALK LENGTH: 7km (4.4 miles)

ASCENT: 192m (630ft)

APPROX. TIME: 2 hours

PARKING: Alwinton Car Park (see above)

CAR FREE: Phone box bus stop at Alwinton village centre

▼ There's a traditional feel to the inside of the pub, which is a great place to hide from the Northumbrian weather.

15

THE DRAKE STONE AT HARBOTTLE & THE STAR INN

— 6.4km (4 miles) —

Looking to get in touch with the wilder side of the north-east? The villages of the Northumberland National Park are where to head. Harbottle is located entirely within the park, which is known as the least populated national park in England, with fewer than 2,000 residents in total. That's an impressive statistic, especially when you consider that the park itself covers 1,049 sq km (405 sq miles) and is also one of the least visited areas of the country. This walk is next door to the Alwin River walk, also included in this book (see page 72), so there's a good opportunity to do both in one day.

As well as being quiet and isolated, this is also ancient countryside. Overlooking the River Coquet, which has been used as a source of power for mills dating back to the 13th century, Harbottle is a quiet and hidden place, a single street of straw-coloured brickwork, unassuming and redolent of an era that still hides itself away in this remote corner of England. Like many of these places, it also plays host to a significant history, with the ruins of Harbottle Castle standing near the river once part of a chain of fortifications designed to protect the area against Scottish invasion.

▶ The Star Inn sits at the heart of Harbottle life.

THE WALK

You can decide to start and end at The Star Inn, in the centre of the village, or at Harbottle Castle Car Park. On the other side of the road, at the car park for Geordy's Nick and West Wood, you join a path uphill across moorland, cairns and rough ground to the Drake Stone, a freestanding boulder said to weigh around 25 tonnes, and a site of significant importance in this area. It is believed the stone was carried here by vast glacial movements, but the quiet air and remote nature of this part of Northumberland lends itself to feeling otherworldly at the best of times, so it's easy to imagine the boulder's mythical importance. In fact, the stone was used in Druidic ritual and ceremonies, and the priestly class of the Celtic people were said to hold it in high regard. With its commanding views over the landscape and great open expanse of sky, many of these ceremonies were likely tied to celestial events.

Continue on past the stone and over the stile, where you'll reach Harbottle Lough – the footpath skirts its edge. You'll be surrounded by boggy ground here but keep going, down towards a fence. Turn right at the fence and you'll be heading towards West Wood. Follow the track and come out of the wood at a gate. Go through the gate and follow the track right to the road.

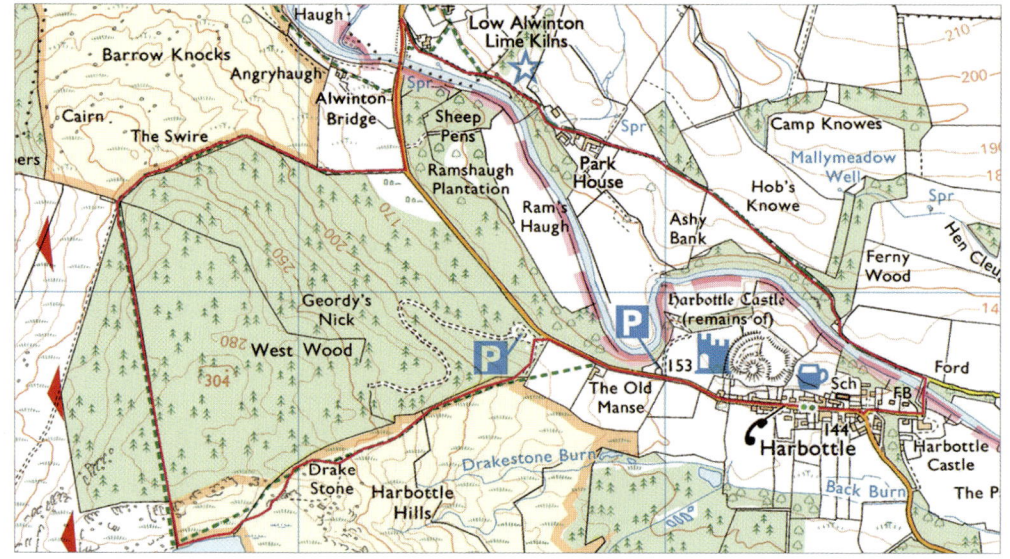

Turn left at the road to Alwinton, and then turn right immediately past the bridge over the river on a minor road. It's signposted Park House. Follow this little road, keeping the river on your right, and as the road ends you'll cross over a stile and through a field with a clearly marked track. Pass a cottage on the right, and you'll soon reach a bridge (again on your right) that will take you back across the River Coquet and into the village.

Step into The Star Inn and you'll be greeted with the cosy country atmosphere of a community meeting

▼ The Drake Stone is of mythical importance, and is said to have special healing powers.

place that serves a variety of functions – you can even stock up on supplies in the shop that's attached to the back, and it's clear that in such a remote location, a rural hub that serves a variety of purposes is vital. The pub was built as a coaching inn over 200 years ago and has recently been refurbished. It has a steady stream of locals and visitors, plus a good tourist information centre too, where you can find out more about the local area. The barn and courtyard out the back provide outdoor seating, and through the year they host a number of community events in this space. Dog owners are especially welcome, and they even serve dog-friendly snacks, 'beer' and ice cream.

THE PUB: The Star Inn, Harbottle, Morpeth, Northumb NE65 7DG
www.thestarinnharbottle.co.uk
01669 650221

START AND END POINT: Harbottle Castle Car Park, 11 Richardson Ln, Harbottle, Morpeth, Northumb NE65 7DG

WALK LENGTH: 6.4km (4 miles)

ASCENT: 208m (682ft)

APPROX. TIME: 1 hour 45 minutes

PARKING: Outside The Star Inn, or at Harbottle Castle (see above)

CAR FREE: First School bus stop in Harbottle

▼ The local shop is attached to the pub at The Star Inn.

16

GREENHAUGH CIRCULAR & HOLLY BUSH INN

— 4km (2.5 miles) —

Walk through the door of Holly Bush Inn and the warmth hits you. Whatever time of day or night, the Victorian black-leaded range that stands over the bar area will most likely be stoked, the routine and habit of keeping it lit and local drinkers warm happily occupying the custodians of this 300-year-old traditional drovers' inn.

Holly Bush Inn is one of the last drovers inns to remain operational in this part of the Northumberland National Park, and the history of the pub and the landscape around it tell a compelling story of the hand-to-mouth existence of farmers and labourers here in times gone by.

Starting and ending at the pub, this walk feels hewn from another time; babbling brooks, verdant woodlands and the pastoral landscape of agricultural Northumberland greet you as you wander through a geography little changed in centuries. It is especially magical in late spring and through summer evenings, as the hay meadows are in full bloom, with the smell of wildflowers, the sound of insect life and the glow of the heat of the day as captivating as the countryside around you.

THE WALK

With your back to the pub door, turn left and follow signs to Sidwood, crossing over the enchanting Tarset Burn, a diminutive tributary of the River Tyne that eventually comes to a dramatic conclusion under the bridges of inner-city Newcastle. After the burn (North-East term for brook or stream), turn left to walk up a straight lane that takes you past the church to Thorneyburn, over a stile on your left and onto a lane that skirts the edge of Thorneyburn Common. Continue straight over the rough common ground, with views back towards the village and across to Hareshaw Common on the other side of the valley. Keep the fence on your

▲ The Holly Bush Inn is situated in the middle of a row of farmer's cottages.

◂ Walking the lanes near Greenhaugh, you're greeted by a wide variety of trees, plants and wildlife.

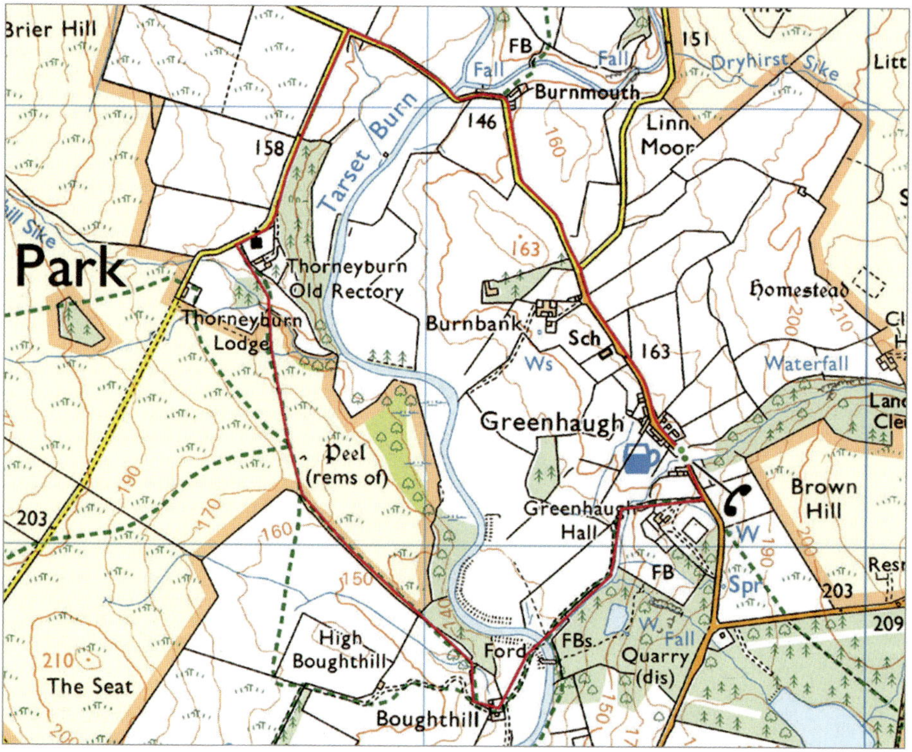

right and keep going until you end up at Boughtill Farm.

Back across Tarset Burn, you will follow this track until it reaches a small lane. At which point, turn right until you emerge at a T-junction. Turn left here, and this will lead back to the village and the pub. The meadows on either side of this part of the walk provide a cacophony of insect and bird sounds at the right time of the year.

The Holly Bush Inn feels like home from home, situated literally among a row of terraced houses right at the heart of the community. 'Lots of buildings around here were built to protect against livestock theft and the border reivers,' the owner of the pub, Lynne, says as

◄ The church at Thorneyburn.

► Farmland around Greenhaugh, viewed from behind traditional north-east walling.

THE PUB: Holly Bush Inn, Greenhaugh, Hexham, Northumb NE48 1PW
🌐 www.hollybushinn.net
☎ 01434 240391

START AND END POINT: Holly Bush Inn (see above)

WALK LENGTH: 4km (2.5 miles)

ASCENT: 79m (259ft)

APPROX. TIME: 1 hour

PARKING: On-street parking available outside Holly Bush Inn (see above)

CAR FREE: No suitable public transport nearby – use Bellingham for nearest bus stops and Tarset Valley Taxis ☎ 01434 240835

▲ The old hearth at the heart of the pub needs stocking up frequently, but rarely goes out.

she's stocking up the bar ready for the evening service. 'Farmers would sleep upstairs and their animals would be protected inside the home downstairs.' The rooms in the inn are named after the seven closest bastle houses – fortified homes in which to store livestock, protecting against theft from these border reivers, raiders along the Anglo-Scottish border, who would go from village to village stealing whatever they could, from animals to valuables, often taking prisoners in the process. These bastle houses are scattered through the landscape here and were mostly built in the 16th/17th centuries to withstand the frequent raids. Black Middens Bastle, which is managed by English Heritage, is the closest to the pub and well worth a visit.

The hearth at the heart of Holly Bush Inn is not only its main selling point and feature, but also a vital source of warmth for the local community, who gather here religiously throughout the year. 'A proper little pub' says the sign above the door, and what it lacks in size, it more than makes up in charm, friendliness and character.

17

KIELDER FOREST & THE PHEASANT INN

— 12.9km (8 miles) —

Under some of the darkest skies in the world lies the Kielder Forest and its groundbreaking observatory. A 'night report' in 2016 highlighted Northumberland's pristine darkness and relatively low levels of light pollution, allowing on clear nights uninterrupted sky-gazing towards thousands of stars, the Milky Way and the Andromeda Galaxy, the nearest galaxy to the Milky Way that lies over 2 million light years away. It's said that more than 85 per cent of the country's population have never seen a truly dark sky – so all the more reason to visit the Kielder Forest.

Armed with a head torch, it's possible to visit Kielder Water and Forest Park by night, and this walk lies close to the observatory, an impressive structure opened in 2008. It now hosts more than 700 astronomical events a year, and is quite rightly considered a jewel in the crown of the British dark skies.

The Pheasant Inn provides an ideal starting point for a circular walk around the Kielder Forest. Beyond Stannersburn, one of the tributaries leading into the North Tyne River, sits the great expanse of Kielder Forest, stretching from the Anglo-Scottish border at the north of Kielder Water to the Hadrian's Wall Path at Haltwhistle in the south. Over the years, the tracks and routes here have been well marked, and there are a plethora of activities on offer, from hiking and cycling to watersports, boating, sailing and camping. It's a playground in nature and one that has to be visited over a number of days to fully appreciate.

THE WALK

There's a generous pub car park at The Pheasant Inn, so you can leave the car here and return to a drink and a hearty lunch when you're back from the forest. From behind the pub, a small lane in Stannersburn leads to a farm track with a gate, gently uphill, with moorland and forest stretching out in front of you.

Continue on this well-marked track before bearing round to the left when you meet a junction in the forest path. The track then takes a sharp right, but keep going until you reach a T-junction. Turn right at the junction, which will lead you west through the forest itself. Once you reach another well-surfaced forest track, turn right towards Kielder Water.

The path then heads gently uphill before lowering over a crest towards Elf Kirk Viewpoint. From here, you can enjoy great views of Kielder Water and the surrounding landscape. Once you're done, continue down towards the main road, crossing over to the other side and joining the waterside path round to the right. This path follows the water's edge, and takes you past a sailing club with public conveniences as well as a big car park and a public viewing point on the peninsula. Keep tracking the path to the east until you reach a lay-by

▶ Kielder Forest is a huge plantation, and one that boasts many easily walkable routes.

THE PUB: The Pheasant Inn, Stannersburn, nr Kielder Water, Hexham, Northumb NE48 1DD
🌐 www.thepheasantinn.com
☎ 01434 240382

START AND END POINT: The Pheasant Inn (see above)

WALK LENGTH: 12.9km (8 miles)

ASCENT: 325m (1,066ft)

APPROX. TIME: 3 hours 10 minutes

PARKING: Outside The Pheasant Inn (see above)

CAR FREE: No nearby public transport – buses available to Bellingham

parking area, at which point go back up to the road, cross it and join the path opposite, back into the forest.

You'll now be walking on the north side of Rotten Moss and the Falstone Moss Nature Reserve. If you keep going here for a couple of kilometres, and don't deviate from this track, you'll emerge at the first junction where you previously kept left. Turn left to retrace your steps back to Stannersburn and The Pheasant Inn.

There's bed and breakfast accommodation at the pub, as well as a generous bar and restaurant area, and a self-catering cottage you can rent should you wish. Dating back to around the mid-1600s, the inn was originally a farmhouse at the hub of this diminutive community. People often gathered here, welcomed by the farmer and his family. Over time it became known locally as 'The Crown Inn', with local amenities based here and mail delivered here for the surrounding regions. In the mid-1980s, the Kershaw family bought the pub and refurbished it, turning it into The Pheasant Inn that stands today.

▼ The view of Kielder Water and the surrounding forest.

18

BLAKEY RIDGE, ROSEDALE RAILWAY & THE LION INN

— 12.6km (7.8 miles) —

The North York Moors are a walking wonderland. Here, you'll find some of the finest landscapes in the UK, with clear, open vistas atop high ridge lines that sweep across remote, windswept moorland.

Situated on Blakely Ridge, a road that dissects the middle of the moors from Farndale to Rosedale, The Lion Inn dates from the 16th century, with stories of it as a meeting point from even earlier – making it one of the oldest surviving inns in the region. It remains family-owned and operated, and was originally a drovers' inn, serving those moving livestock across the moors. The views from here are sublime; standing at an elevation of 404m (1,325ft) above sea level, this makes it the highest pub in the North York Moors, and this walk takes in the best of the Rosedale area in which it sits.

THE WALK

After enjoying the views from The Lion Inn car park, head south with the pub on your right and look for a sign on your left that points to the direction of Rosedale Railway south. This track once served as the route of the Rosedale Railway. Opened in 1861, with the primary purpose of transporting ironstone from the Rosedale mines to the steel furnaces in the Teesside area, the railway stretched for about 20km (12.5 miles), running across the moorland to the Ingleby Incline and onward to Battersby Junction. The Ingleby Incline was one of the steepest pieces of railway in the UK and was

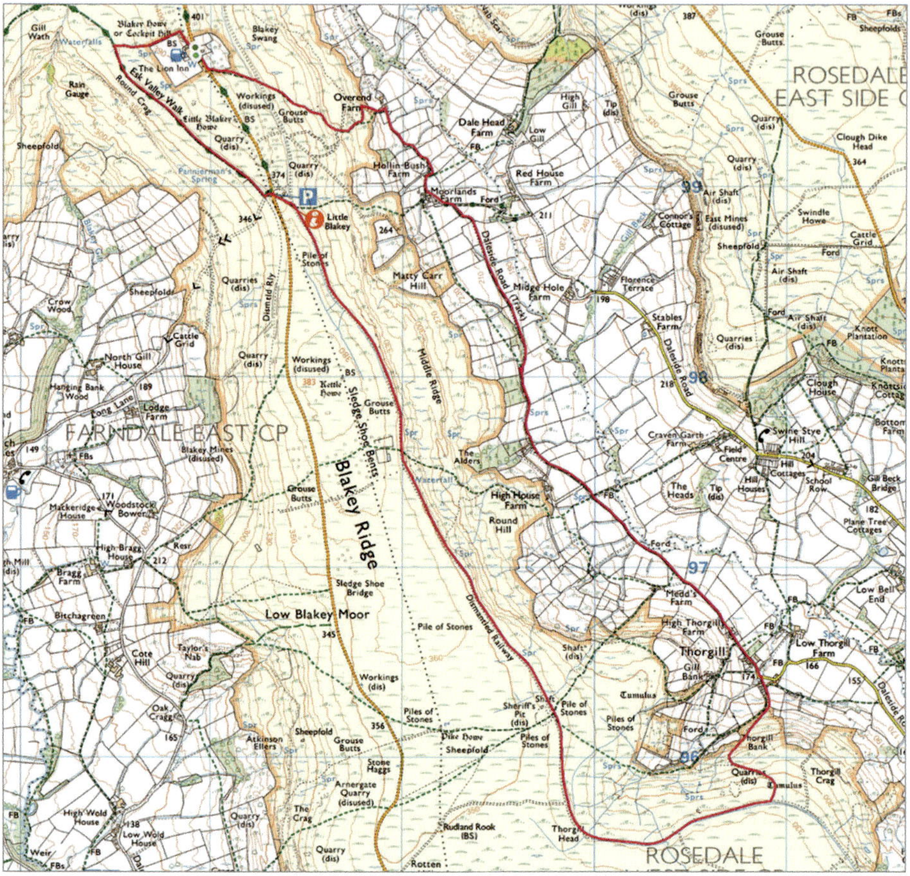

▲ The Lion Inn at Blakey Ridge sits highs up on the hills, and cuts a remote figure on the North York Moors.

operated using a cable system to haul wagons up and down.

Before long, you'll reach a lane that leads down the hill to Overend Farm. Pass through the farm, turn right and continue to Hollin Bush Farm and then after that Moorlands Farm, following the track in a southerly direction, turning left at Moorlands Farm and then immediately right at the gate onto a farm track. You can follow Daleside Road, a farm track, for about 3.2km (2 miles), with other large farms to your left and right, before you reach the agricultural hamlet of Thorgill.

Continue walking through Thorgill, and as the road bears round to the left, take a footpath climbing up onto Thorgill Bank. There's an obvious route through the moors that leads to the old Rosedale Railway line again. Turn right, and follow this disused line for a few kilometres, heading west initially, and then bearing round to the north. From the line, there are superb views down to the valley on your right and the exposed moorland on your left.

> **THE PUB:** The Lion Inn, Blakey Ridge, High Blakey, York, N. Yorks YO62 7LQ
> 🌐 www.lionblakey.co.uk
> ☎ 01751 417320
>
> **START AND END POINT:** The Lion Inn (see above)
>
> **WALK LENGTH:** 12.6km (7.8 miles)
>
> **ASCENT:** 279m (915ft)
>
> **APPROX. TIME:** 3 hours
>
> **PARKING:** Car park at The Lion Inn (see above)
>
> **CAR FREE:** Bus outside the pub, route M6 from York to Danby

▼ The walking routes around the North York Moors are a hiker's paradise, and are especially beautiful when the heather is in full colour.

▲ Looking down across the farmland of the North York Moors, from high above.

Soon, you'll reach Little Blakey, with an information board and a left turn leading to a small car park. Take this path, cross the road and head down the moorland on the opposite side, turning immediately right to continue a northbound trajectory on the Esk Valley Walk, with the remoteness of the Farndale Valley on your left. After about 1.3km (0.75 mile) on this route, you'll see a path right, which takes you to the back of The Lion Inn. After about 500m (1,640ft) you'll reach the road again and The Lion Inn on your right.

There's a truly rustic atmosphere to The Lion Inn, and it feels as remote on the inside as it does on the outside, but in a way that is cosy and protected from the elements. There are 13 bedrooms here, and being so high, the pub is no stranger to snow, ice and the howling elements this exposed moorland territory throws at it. In contrast to the solitude of the moor, there's often a roaring fire and good conversation on offer here, and it's especially evocative on a cold winter's day, the air tinged with the scent of damp peatland and wood smoke.

19

HOLE OF HORCUM & THE HORSESHOE INN

— 12km (7.5 miles) —

One of the most picturesque national parks in the UK, the North York Moors cover 1,430 sq km (554 sq miles) and have the added benefit of being situated in a lesser visited part of the UK. Like much of the east coast in this book, from Northumberland down to Lincolnshire and Norfolk, there is an isolated, seldom visited charm to the area, and even in the busiest spots you're likely to find time to yourself, as well as corners that feel rarely trodden and lesser explored.

An immense variety of landscapes exist here, a combination of heather-covered uplands, deep dales, ancient woodlands and dramatic coastline, and the area also houses many archeological sites, from burial grounds to standing stones. This

▼ The Hole of Horcum is a naturally formed 'cauldron' and dips down 120m (400ft) into the North York Moorland landscape.

walk takes in one of the area's most famous features, the Hole of Horcum, often described as a 'giant's cauldron'. The naturally occurring bowl-shaped depression is about 122m (400ft) deep and nearly 1.6km (1 mile) across and, according to local legend, it was formed when a giant named Wade scooped up a handful of earth to throw at his wife during an argument. Geologically, it's a classic example of a 'dry valley', formed by the gradual erosion of the limestone bedrock.

THE WALK

From the symmetrical village of Levisham, with pretty Yorkshire cottages lining either side of the road, you'll find The Horseshoe Inn directly in front of you – a small patch of village green grass acting as its charming pub garden.

Follow Braygate Lane to the left of the pub and when the paved road bears round to the left, continue straight on along the rough path that takes you to the edge of Levisham Moor. Following the edge of a field, continue to a point where a few paths converge. Continue straight ahead here, up a slight hill to the north-west.

At the top of this hill, follow a path along the other side of the elevation round to the right, down to the ruined Skelton Tower, which offers a fantastic view into Newtondale and over the track of the North Yorkshire Moors Railway. Built around 1830 by Robert Skelton,

rector of Levisham, he is thought to have used it as overnight lodgings after a day's shooting on the moors. The grassy headland is a wonderful spot for a picnic, and you'll often hear the whistle of the steam trains below, which adds to its evocative, old-world charm.

From the tower, follow the path to its right to continue along the side of the hill, keeping the Pickering Beck and the railway line to your left. On the crest of the hill sits the relatively easygoing Tabular Hills Walk path, which you can join should you wish, but in any case, keep going until you reach a sharp bend in the road at Gallow's Dyke.

Follow a path that heads south into the Hole of Horcum, and appreciate the steep-sided cliff-like formations above you that form the sides of this natural amphitheater. Cross Levisham Beck and keep going past an isolated farm building on an obvious route on the moorland, and past these buildings, keep right when you have a choice of paths to keep the woodland area on your left-hand side. At the bottom of the valley, the path

THE PUB: The Horseshoe Inn, Main St, Levisham, Pickering, N. Yorks YO18 7NL
🌐 www.horseshoelevisham.co.uk
📞 01751 460240

START AND END POINT: The Horseshoe Inn (see above)

WALK LENGTH: 12km (7.5 miles)

ASCENT: 308m (1,010ft)

APPROX. TIME: 3 hours

PARKING: Car park behind The Horseshoe Inn (see above)

CAR FREE: Lane End bus stop in Lockton – 840 Coastliner route from York and Leeds to Whitby

▼ The Hole of Horcum from above, with its large, natural amphitheatre.

then crosses the beck again before rising through a patch of trees and scrubland, with the water on your left. Keep following this path through the woodland area as it bears around to the right, at which point you'll be nearing the village of Levisham again. You'll eventually appear out of the tree-covered area at the southern edge of the village, at which point turn right and follow the straight road back to the pub.

The pub's history is closely tied to the agricultural roots of Levisham, and many of the buildings here have existed in some form or another since medieval times. The Horseshoe Inn itself dates back to the 16th century, when it served as a coaching inn, providing respite for travellers making their way across the remote moorland. They have rooms and cottages you can stay in, both within the pub and in nearby farm cottages, and the menu here is much celebrated. For railway enthusiasts who want to sample the famous steam trains on the North Yorkshire Moors Railway, Levisham station is close by.

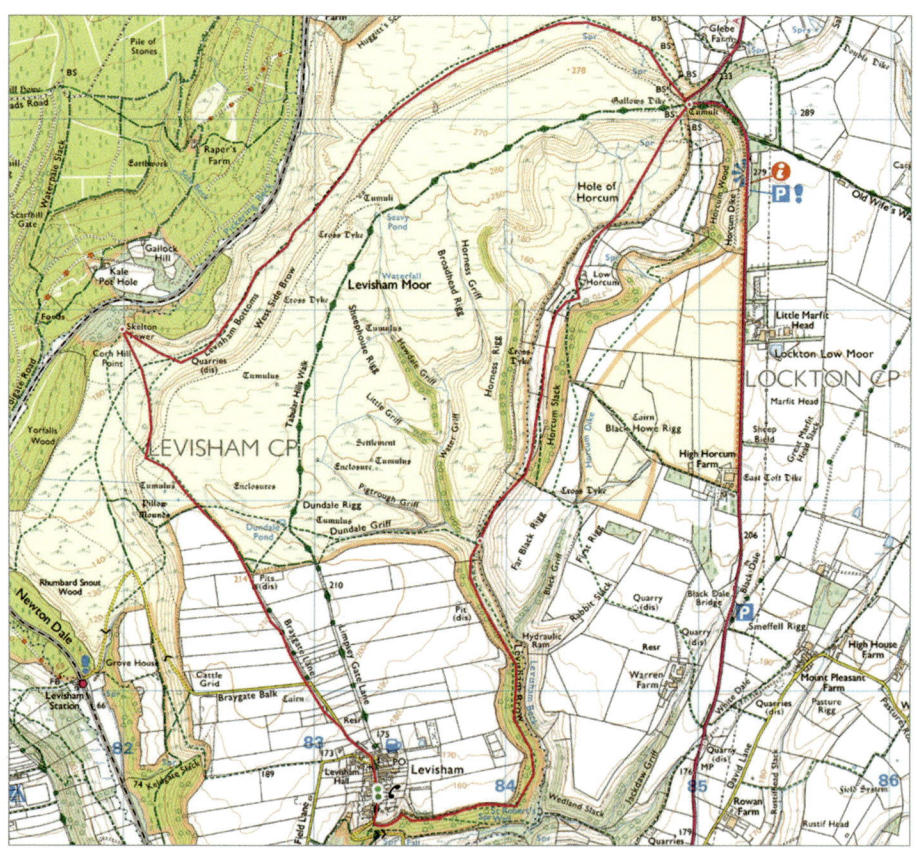

20

KILBURN WHITE HORSE & THE FAUCONBERG

— 14.3km (8.9 miles) —

The curiously named Fauconberg was christened as such thanks to this village's long-lasting legacy. The Fauconberg family, who were gifted the land around here by Henry VIII, took up ownership of a village that has roots as far back as the Domesday Book, where it is recorded as 'Cuche-wolde', which suggests a name derived from Old English meaning 'Cuhu's forest clearing'. It's a personal title, which implies individual ownership, but other records show the village referred to as 'Cucvalt', which means 'Cuckoo's Wood'.

Whatever its name and history, there's no denying its glorious location. Honey-coloured stone buildings line the street in this village, with the huge St Michael's Church offering an excellent example of one of the few churches in England with an octagonal tower. The church is closely associated with Laurence Sterne, author of *The Life and Opinions of Tristram Shandy, Gentleman*. Sterne was the vicar of Coxwold from 1760 until his death in 1768, and is buried in the churchyard. Opposite the church, a little way up the lane sits Shandy Hall, where he lived, and the house and garden is often open for visits thanks to the Laurence Sterne Trust.

▼ The White Horse at Kilburn is visible from miles around.

THE PUB: The Fauconberg, Thirsk Bank, Coxwold, York, N. Yorks YO61 4AD
🌐 www.fauconbergarms.com
📞 01347 868214

START AND END POINT: The Fauconberg (see above)

WALK LENGTH: 14.3km (8.9 miles)

ASCENT: 315m (1,033ft)

APPROX. TIME: 3 hours 30 minutes

PARKING: Outside The Fauconberg (see above)

CAR FREE: The Fauconberg bus stop, situated next to the pub

THE WALK

Past Shandy Hall, a short way up Thirsk Bank, sits a little right-hand turning through a gate that leads you into neighbouring fields – look out for the fingerpost sign next to the road's national speed limit signs. Continue on the path round the fields until you reach a small lane – turn right here uphill past a collection of rustic farm buildings. It's very much working land around here, and as you descend again the road turns a sharp right, still heading downhill.

Follow the path straight ahead through a wooded area, leaving the road, until you reach a track for Weatherill Barn. Follow this north to the road at High Kilburn.

Turn left at the road and follow it initially uphill, past the sign for the village and a street of large, fine houses surrounding a village green. Keep going past the houses on the lane, going downhill before carrying on through a gate when the road bends sharply to the left, following yellow waymarker

▲ The Fauconberg sits at the heart of the community and is frequently voted one of the best pubs to visit in this area of north Yorkshire.

signs. This enables you to cut through fields before you emerge by the church, turning right on Carr Lane and leaving the village behind you.

As you head north on Carr Lane, the massive White Horse comes into view. This is the largest white horse chalk figure in England; it measures 97m (318ft) long and 67m (220ft) high and covers about 0.6ha (1.6 acres) of the hillside in front of you. A community effort, it was created in 1857 by a local schoolmaster and his students, who were inspired by the chalk figures of southern England. It's so distinctive from the air and the surrounding areas, that during the Second World War, it was covered over with netting to prevent enemy aircraft using it as a navigation marker.

Carr Lane bends round to the right, and when you reach a fork in the road, follow the brown sign to the White Horse. A short way down this road, you'll see a drive on your left, which you can follow to join up with the path through the wooded area that sits below the horse. Turn right when you can, and find your way up to the stunning views above the horse, with huge vistas stretching south towards the city of York.

From here, you can find your way to the White Horse Car Park, and continue down the hill back towards Carr Lane again. When you reach the junction in the road, instead of going back the way you came, turn left across undulating countryside on Oldstead Road, turning right at the junction with River Road, following signs back to High Kilburn 1.2km (0.75 miles) away. This road will soon lead you to where you emerged from the fields near Weatherill Barn. You can turn left and follow your tracks from here back to Coxwold.

Back at The Fauconberg, you'll be greeted by an extensive B&B and restaurant area, but also an intimate low-ceilinged bar with plenty of local ales to choose from. They also have a decent set of picnic benches out the front and a great garden.

▼ The distinctive white horse at Kilburn is instantly recognisable, and features a gliding club above.

CENTRAL & NORTHERN

It is said that within the central areas of England, you can feel the heartbeat of the country. From the gentle, rolling hills of the Cotswolds in the south, to the bustling urban sprawl of Birmingham and up towards the industrialised north. Central England is a region where rural beauty is mixed with industrial innovation, and where traditional rural life coexists with modern multicultural urban sprawls.

The Cotswolds, with its iconic rolling hills and picturesque villages, is one of the most recognisable landscapes in Central England. Prosperous hubs of the wool trade, as highlighted by the walk around The Woolpack Inn in Slad (see page 135), lie tucked among quiet, hidden trails. Away from the crowds, you can still discover enchanting parts of this landscape, dotted with honey-coloured cottages.

As you move further north, the landscape becomes more varied, with the introduction of the Peak District. The rugged moorlands, deep dales and limestone gorges are popular with hikers and climbers, and as one of England's

oldest National Parks, the Peak District promises plenty of adventure for intrepid visitors. Walks around Kinder Scout (see page 104) showcase the area's wild side, and the Bugsworth Basin walk near Chinley (see page 108) provides insight into the region's extensive canal network.

Originally built to transport goods such as coal and iron, the canals played a crucial role in the region's industrial development. Today, these waterways have become popular for leisure boating and walking, offering a scenic retreat from the hustle of nearby cities – a perfect spot for visitors who want to stay a few days and explore at a slower pace.

Near Stoke-on-Trent, the Yew Tree Inn (see page 112) is a delightful escape from the modern world, with an excellent walk around the area's quarries that were once at the heart of the country's pottery industry. Further west, in the charming land of the Welsh Marches lies Craswall and The Bull's Head (see page 129), an ideal spot to experience not only a fantastic pub and ingredient-led cooking, but the source of an excellent example of local, regenerative farming.

21

EDALE CIRCULAR & THE OLD NAGS HEAD

— 11.3km (7 miles) —

From on high, it would be an understatement to say that there's a feeling of topographical significance as you descend into the valley that plays host to the start of England's first and most famous long-distance walk, the Pennine Way.

As you turn left off the A6, the small lane, like so many others in the Peak District, narrows and is fringed by dry stone walls and hedgerows that have stood here as long as the byways themselves. As you pass Mam Tor, the view opens up to one of the most impressive in England; a panorama of peaks with ancient villages peppering the landscape, misty fields and muddy farm lanes rising high up the hillsides. Whether you're visiting in summer or winter, there's no doubting the hardship once felt here, which can be seen across this landscape. The rigours of community life in such a high, remote location are there for all to see in the farms that stick to the windswept tors and surrounding hillsides.

It comes as a surprise, then, that once you reach Edale you find a village and community as perfectly formed as it is. A church, small school, café and village shop border a lane that runs through the village and into the remote wilds of the Peaks. There's a train station where trains from across the region stop, including from major nearby cities such as Sheffield and Liverpool, which explains why on any day of the week Edale is an outdoor enthusiast's paradise and walkers can be seen flocking here from all corners of the world.

▶ The Old Nags Head has been welcoming hikers from the surrounding hills for many years, and features a large dining area and beer garden.

THE WALK

The Old Nags Head pub sits at the heart of the village, and provides the main sustenance to many of these walkers. Being in the centre of the village, it's also the start and end point of the walk. Starting opposite the pub, take the lane signposted 'the Pennine Way' to the very start of the trail – a sign marks the point at which this 431km (268 mile) route begins. Through the gate, the path narrows before climbing up to an open field. Keep bearing left, marked by the stones that cross the field, keeping the high peak of Grindslow Knoll on your right. Before long, you'll be gaining altitude, but first, enjoy the relative serenity of the lowland fields and farmland as you progress towards the small farming community of Upper Booth.

Keep the hill on your right and take the left-hand path each time there's an option, and before long you'll reach a collection of farm buildings. Upper Booth is managed by the National Trust and there's a campsite here too for those with wilder tendencies. It's one of the best places to stay for Kinder Scout and

▲ The official start of the Pennine Way is marked with a discreet green sign.

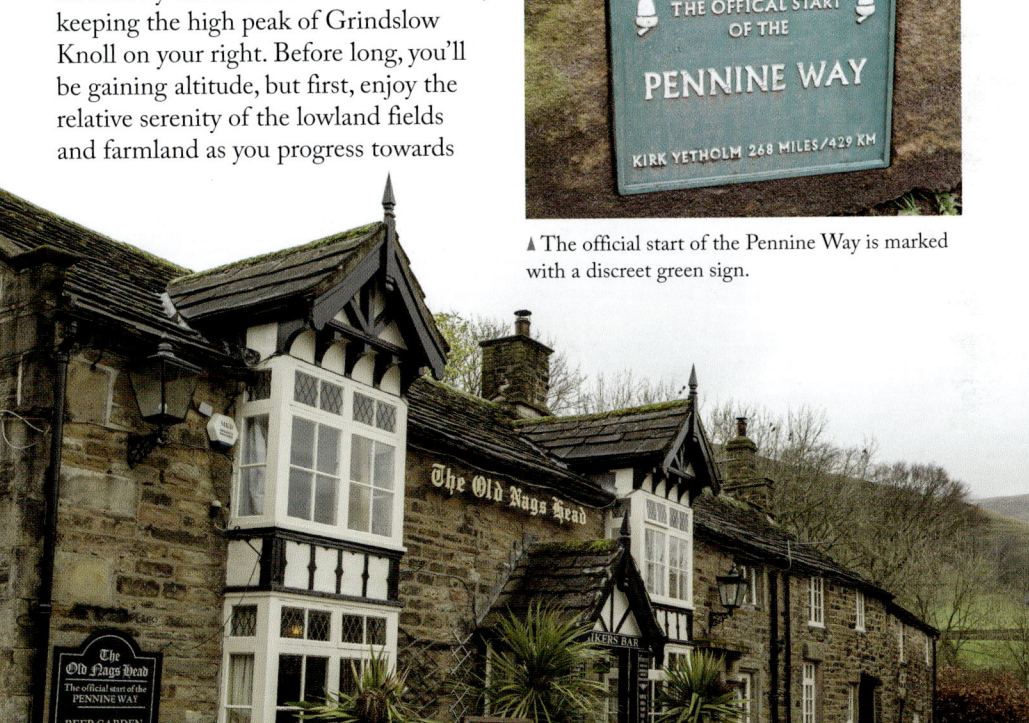

▲ The views behind you as you start climbing up Jacob's Ladder, get increasingly more impressive.

the surrounding walks, but be warned that flat spaces are at a premium.

By now, you'll have the highest parts of Kinder Scout and the surrounding hills in full view, as the farm cottages get smaller and signs of civilisation diminish. Through a gate past the farm buildings, the path becomes a dirt track as you walk past some holiday cottages and on to Jacob's Ladder, the famous start of the ascent to Kinder Scout.

Jacob's Ladder is an aerobic test, there's no question, but it pays to stop every few metres to admire the spectacle that's getting increasingly impressive behind you. As you ascend, the valley floor comes into view, and with Brown Knoll on your right and Grindslow Knoll on your left, you'll be left wondering how many prettier views there are in England. As the intense climb lessens, the steps stop and the gravel path resumes, you'll now be nearing the top of Kinder Scout and the atmosphere takes on a wilder air. Standing at 636m (2,087ft) above sea level, Kinder Scout is the highest point in the Peak District and the highest moorland plateau in the UK. It's primarily composed of gritstone, a type of sandstone that forms rugged and rocky terrain, and at the Edale Rocks you can climb to

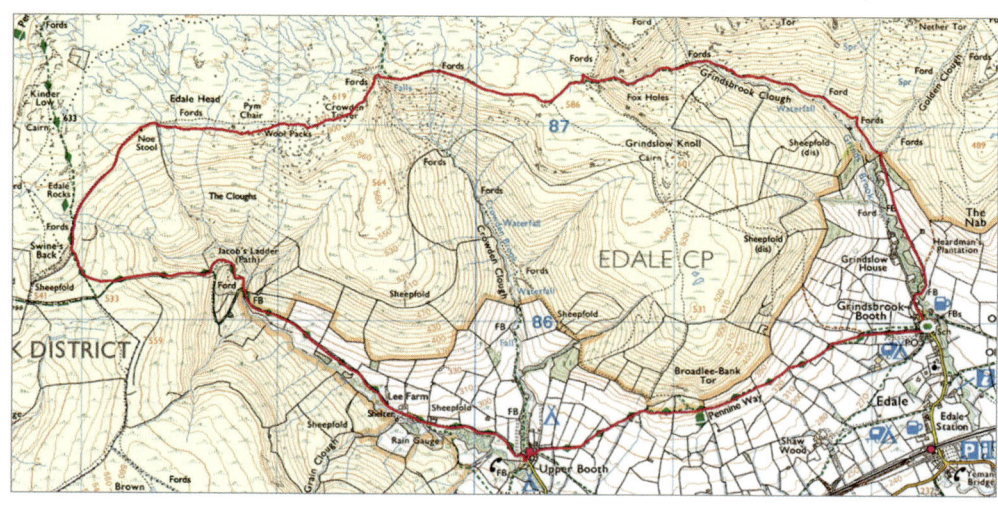

get a better 360-degree view of the surrounding landscape. Manchester and Liverpool sit to your immediate west, and to the east across much of the rest of the surrounding high landscape, the lights of Sheffield are buried among the moorland.

After admiring the view, continue past the rocks on your left and head north, taking the smaller right-hand option when the path forks and continuing slightly downhill. You'll now be crossing onto Edale Moor past Noe Stool and Pym Chair, two impressive clifftop formations that offer impressive views across the valley but are not for the fainthearted. Watch your step.

The plateau here is characterised by extensive peat bogs, so it can be tough going on the hiking boots, but bogs vitally store carbon and provide habitat for unique plant and animal species, which is part of why this area is so geographically protected.

Past the Wool Packs and Crowden Tower, the path becomes more obvious again and there are fewer peat bogs around – you're back on the Pennine Way and the path now continues across the highest areas of the moorland before you begin your descent back into Edale. At the Fox Holes, marked on the OS Map by the decrease in space between the contour lines, it pays to take extra care. This is the only tricky part of the walk as you descend a steep valley across boulders. Keep the brook on your left to start with and you can't go far wrong – the path soon flattens, and it becomes more manageable as you follow the now larger Grinds Brook down to the top of Edale and back into the village.

At The Old Nags Head, as you pass under the entrance to the 'Hiker's Bar', you'll be greeted with a menu that caters well to hungry walkers. Food is served from 12pm to 8pm with a walk-in service that doesn't take bookings – perfect for weary legs to recharge. The expansive dining halls of the pub date back to 1577, with suitably cosy snugs and roaring fires to dry your socks off at the end of a hard day on the hills.

The area gained notoriety in 1932 when it became the site of the Mass Trespass, a pivotal moment in the struggle for access to the countryside. This event played a significant role in the establishment of national parks and the right to roam in the UK, and looking back on the landscape in which you've just walked, you'll be hard pushed to think of a better site in which to appreciate the surrounding environment.

THE PUB: The Old Nags Head, Grindsbrook Booth, Edale, Derbs S33 7ZD
www.the-old-nags-head.co.uk
01433 670291

START AND END POINT: The Old Nags Head (see above)

WALK LENGTH: 11.3km (7 miles)

ASCENT: 512m (1,680ft)

APPROX. TIME: 3 hours 30 minutes

PARKING: Edale Car Park, Water Meadows, Hope Rd, Edale, Hope Valley, Derbs S33 7ZQ

CAR FREE: Edale train station, services from Manchester Piccadilly and Sheffield

22

BUGSWORTH BASIN & THE OLD HALL INN

— 7.9km (4.9 miles) —

If storybooks made Peak District hamlets, the little collection of buildings known as Whitehough, next to the village of Chinley, would take centre stage. Its picturesque streets on the borders of the Peak District bely its relatively urban location, with Manchester just a short drive away and the larger towns of Chapel-en-le-Frith and Buxton 20 minutes down the road. This walk and The Old Hall Inn make a perfect stopping-off point as part of larger excursions into the deeper reaches of the peaks, but the area itself provides an impressive array of hiking opportunities to sample some fantastic views, with a selection of routes that offer a range of difficulty levels for hikers of all abilities.

There's an abundance of choice in Whitehough, as two award-winning country inns – both run by the same people – are located directly next to each other and provide an excellent base to start a day. The Old Hall Inn is the larger of the two pubs, with The Paper Mill Inn across the road offering a more rustic, industrial feel, with fresh pizza, pies and pop-up menus from local producers and chefs from the area. Like many well-established pubs in the region, there's a feeling of old grandeur and prosperity in their architecture – they have a sense of location and place that, fortunately, any renovation and decoration work has supported rather than diminished. The dining areas, bar and rooms here have been smartened up just enough, but not so much as to take away from what feels like a cosy, unpretentious and friendly environment to base yourself.

▶ The Old Hall Inn is a unique and charming building, and a quintessential country pub that hasn't been tampered with.

THE WALK

Begin your day at the car park for The Old Hall Inn, which is situated around the back of the pub. Turn around, pass the pub garden on your left and turn right up the hill, with The Paper Mill Inn straight ahead of you. Cross the A6 road and take the first right onto Eccles Terrace. At the end of this road, take the path to the left, up a driveway, keeping along the footpath when the drive leads into the property. Turn left at the lane, before bearing right at the crossroads across rolling fields towards Eccles Road. From here, without going through the gate to the road, you can reach the summit of Eccles Hill, with views down to Combs Reservoir and the surrounding High Peaks.

Back down from Eccles Hill, turn right on the road until you reach the little hamlet of Hilltop, passing Ollerenshaw Hall and following the same lane until it reaches Horwich Farm and turns a sharp left. Keep following the path straight ahead, before turning right and then immediately left over a stile, following a track along the edge of a field, past the old cricket ground and downhill towards the town of Whaley Bridge.

You'll reach the new cricket ground on your left, at which point turn right and head north up through Bings Wood, bearing round to the right after the trees and through open fields, following the line of sight until you reach a T-junction in the path. Turn left here, and head down towards Buxworth and the Bugsworth Basin. Turn left when you reach the road, and cross the A6 towards the canal basin.

You're now deep within English industrial heritage; the Bugsworth Basin was built as the terminus of the Peak Forest Canal, and was once the largest and busiest inland port on the narrow canal system anywhere in England. During its heyday, limestone was exchanged here from canal boats to a tramway, and the

▲ Bugsworth Basin was once the centre of industrial activity, and is now a maintained and restored heritage site.

site was restored to its present condition thanks largely to a campaign by the Inland Waterways Protection Society and the Waterway Recovery Group. Funding to restore the site came from British Waterways, and in 2005, the basin opened once again to public canal traffic. You can find out more at the small exhibit here, and by visiting the Bugsworth Basin Heritage Trust website.

Leave the basin on the easterly side and pick up the Peak Forest Tramway Trail, passing the Navigation Inn on the left and walking on what was the site of the early horse-drawn industrial railway here, opened in the 1790s. After about 1.6km (1 mile) on the tramway route, after passing an industrial complex on your left, you're back in Whitehough – turn right up the hill to reach The Old Hall Inn.

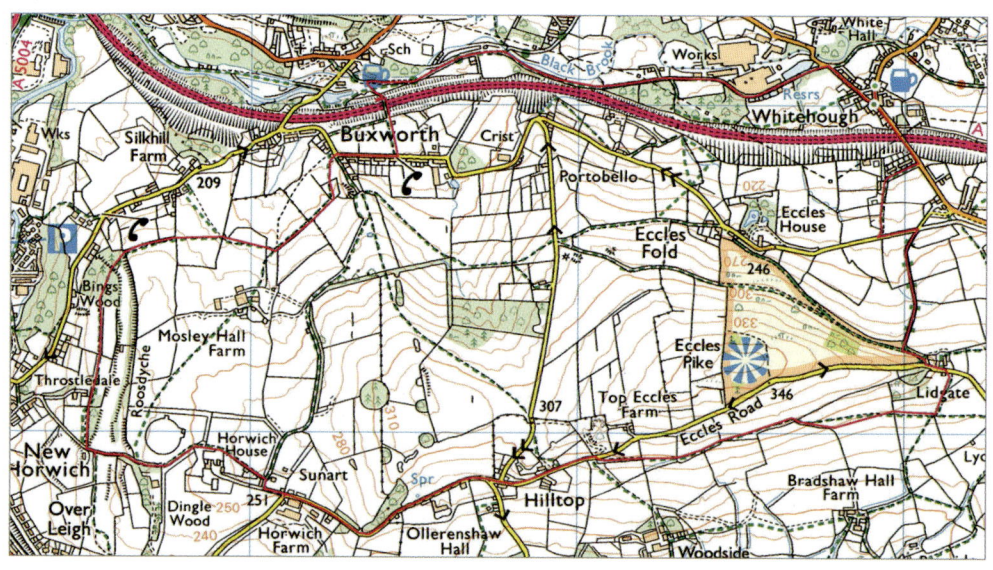

THE PUB: The Old Hall Inn, Whitehough, Chinley, High Peak, Derbs SK23 6EJ
🌐 www.old-hall-inn.co.uk
📞 01663 750529

START AND END POINT: The Old Hall Inn (see above)

WALK LENGTH: 7.9km (4.9 miles)

ASCENT: 197m (646ft)

APPROX. TIME: 2 hours

PARKING: Car park behind The Old Hall Inn (see above)

CAR FREE: Leaden Knowle bus stop on the B6062, just north of the pub. Or Chinley train station for services from Sheffield and Manchester

23

CAULDON & YEW TREE INN

— 9.5km (5.9 miles) —

Located near Stoke-on-Trent, it'll be no surprise to many that Cauldon's history is deeply rooted within the British pottery industry. This area is home to Cauldon Ceramics, the maker of the original 'Brown Betty' teapot that adorned millions of kitchen shelves throughout the 20th century, manufacturing still plays a big role in the area.

To this day, this is quarrying land. The Cauldon Low quarries, located near the village, are some of the oldest limestone quarries in England, having been operational since the late 17th century. This landscape is characterised by the remnants of this large-scale activity, with sizeable, excavated areas, spoil heaps and now-reclaimed land that has been turned into ecological sites for nature. These features have shaped the local geography and made it a fascinating place for a walk.

Given the area's history of making things, it'll also come as no surprise that the Yew Tree Inn, according to their website, is 'an Aladdin's Cave of antiques, curios, music machines and motorcycles'. They're not joking: as soon as you walk through the door, you'll see an eclectic mix of almost anything you can think of, from 'a pair of Queen Victoria's stockings, a 3,000-year-old Grecian urn, a Penny Farthing and an array of unusual musical instruments'. The seating is equally interesting, with antique benches, pews and settles – it's a treasure trove of old-fashioned historical charm.

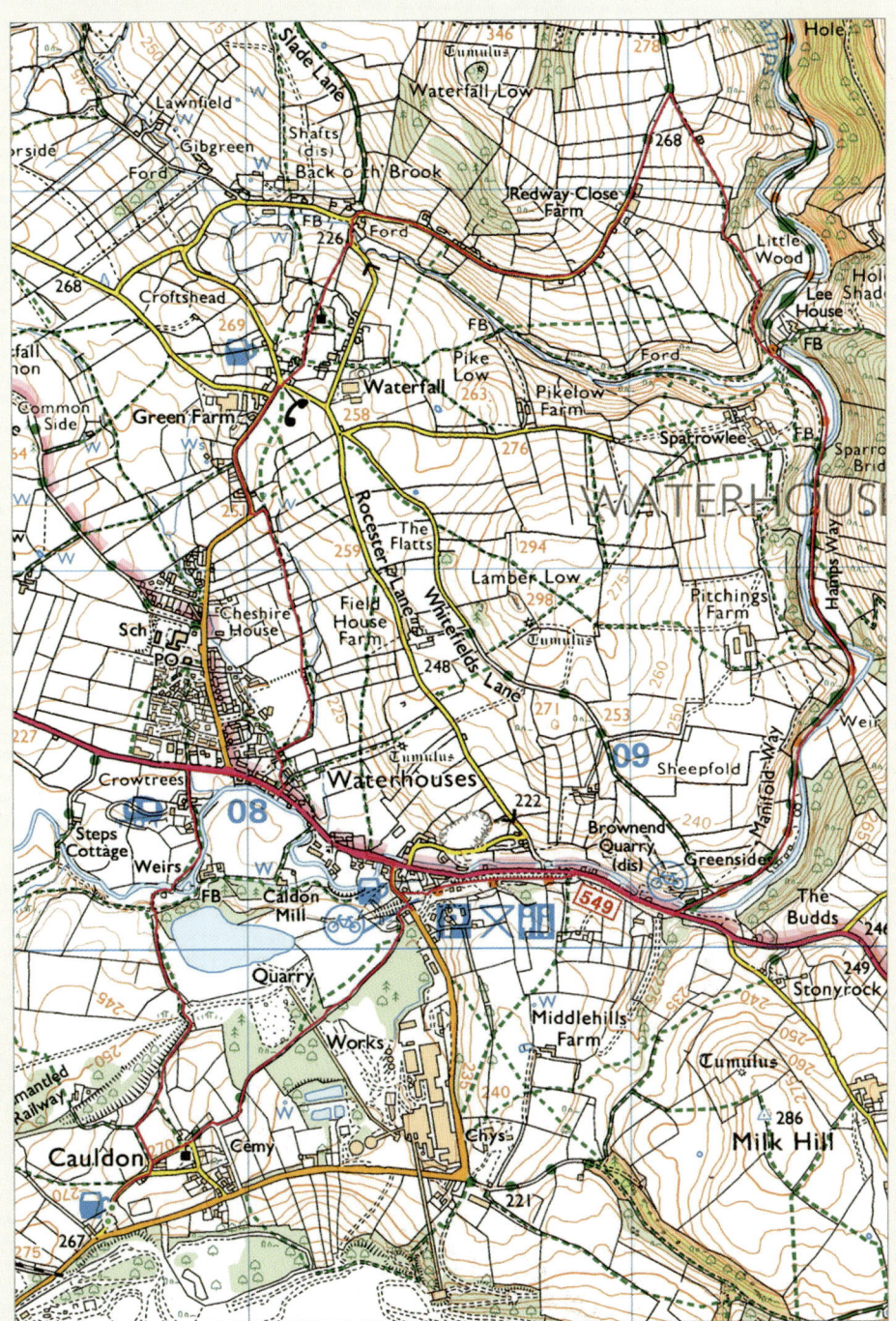

THE WALK

When you're ready to set off, leave on the road behind the pub heading north-east, turning left at a collection of houses, then immediately straight, onto a farm track. This path bends right, through a field, until you reach a large quarry beneath you – cross over above the quarry paths towards a large pool, and then cross the River Hamps, keeping to the right of a caravan park until you reach a large A road.

Turn right at the A road and keep to the pavement, before turning left as the road starts to go downhill, following a public footpath sign past a double garage. From here, follow the signs left and then right again before the path emerges onto fields, negating the need to walk into anyone's private driveway. Heading north, the route passes playing fields and crosses neighbouring fields until it takes a sharp left and emerges onto Waterfall Lane, with a large house to your right and great views across to surrounding farmland. Turn right and walk past the attractive farm buildings, continuing on the road until you reach the pretty hamlet at Green Farm and a red post box.

Continue straight here, past the phone box and down towards a house, which you pass on your left, heading straight for St James & St Bartholomew Church. Pass the church and continue through the fields beside it, following

▼ The winding lanes on this walk provide an insight into the industrial heartland of England.

the route before coming out at the aptly named Back o' th' Brook. Here, you'll ford said brook over a little bridge and turn right past a no-through-road sign. Continue along this lane and it'll eventually peter out at Redway Close Farm, but keep going until you reach the top of the hill, before turning right and heading downhill towards the valley to pick up the Manifold Way.

The Manifold Way runs alongside the river, and you can follow this path all the way back to the A523, emerging onto the road next to the road sign for Waterhouses. Turn right and stay on the pavement for a few hundred metres

> **THE PUB:** Yew Tree Inn, 3 Church Ln, Cauldon, Stoke-on-Trent, Staffs ST10 3EJ
> www.yewtreeantiquepub.co.uk
> 01538 309876
>
> **START AND END POINT:** Yew Tree Inn (see above)
>
> **WALK LENGTH:** 9.5km (5.9 miles)
>
> **ASCENT:** 207m (679ft)
>
> **APPROX. TIME:** 2 hours 15 minutes
>
> **PARKING:** Car park at Yew Tree Inn (see above)
>
> **CAR FREE:** Church Lane bus stop near the pub, with routes to Leek and Ashbourne

▲ The cement works between Cauldon and Waterhouses produces up to one million tonnes of cement a year to be used across the country.

CENTRAL & NORTHERN

▲ The Yew Tree Inn is a captivating place celebrating antiquity and charm.

before bearing left away from the traffic and onto the cycle path. Once you reach a small road, cross this and keep on the footpath, with the quarry to your left, all the way back to Cauldon and the pub.

If you strike it lucky with your timing, back at the pub, you'll be able to enjoy one of the many events they put on throughout the year. It's especially popular with classic car and motorcycle rallies, and camping is available in their garden. Live music is popular, too. As well as the amazing interior, they also pride themselves on their real ales, locally-made pork pies, traditional pub games (including darts, table skittles and shove ha'penny) and a player piano. There's also a distinct, and thankful, lack of Sky Sports or even a TV. If you're looking for old-fashioned, heart-of-England charm, the Yew Tree Inn will be a happy blast from the past.

▼ The pub is a popular spot for vintage car and bike meets, and there's a generous garden and camping area at the back.

24

TEALBY LOOP & THE KINGS HEAD

— 6.8km (4.2 miles) —

There are some rural parts of England where you know you're going to meet crowds of visitors, and then there is the Lincolnshire Wolds. Unlike its otherwise flat neighbours, the Wolds is famous for its blend of rolling hills, ancient woodland and stone cottages that arguably resemble the very essence of rural England. In fact, this land is the highest ground in eastern England between Kent and Yorkshire, but it's not well known, and there's an undeniably undiscovered, protected atmosphere down every narrow lane.

Calm and deep peace on this high world,
And on these dews that drench the furze,
And all the silvery gossamers
That twinkle into green and gold.

As Alfred Tennyson's 'In Memoriam' describes above, there's a deep sense of calm and tranquillity here. The travel writer Stephen McClarence describes the Wolds as a 'secret rhapsody in green' and, largely thanks to their location on the edge of the East Midlands, this landscape is protected by anyone who is simply passing through. From the perspective of a tourist, it is in many ways on the road to nowhere, and the whole region has been superbly preserved.

▲ The church at Tealby contains many memorials to members of the Tennyson family.

THE WALK

The village of Tealby, the start of our walk and home to The Kings Head, can be traced back as far as the 5th century. Originally a milling village, it became famous in the 19th century as the home of the Tealby Hoard, a collection of more than 5,000 silver pennies found that date from medieval England. At All Saints Church, a 12th-century church with memorials to the Tennyson family inside, walk through the graveyard and then turn left along the road once you reach it. After about 90m (100 yards) you'll reach a right-hand turn signposted the Viking Way to Walesby – follow this across a field, with wide open skies spanning out in front of you.

You can follow yellow markers for the Viking Way at this point along the edge of fields, and at a gateway, continue uphill and bear round to a path on the right at the next yellow marker as you skirt to the right of Castle Farm and through a small patch of woodland known as Bedlam plantation. Continue through the woodland and on to Risby Manor, following the route as it dips downhill and up the other side of the valley. Go through the next field and onto the path to the church at Walesby.

► The village of Tealby may be quiet, but it is teeming with character.

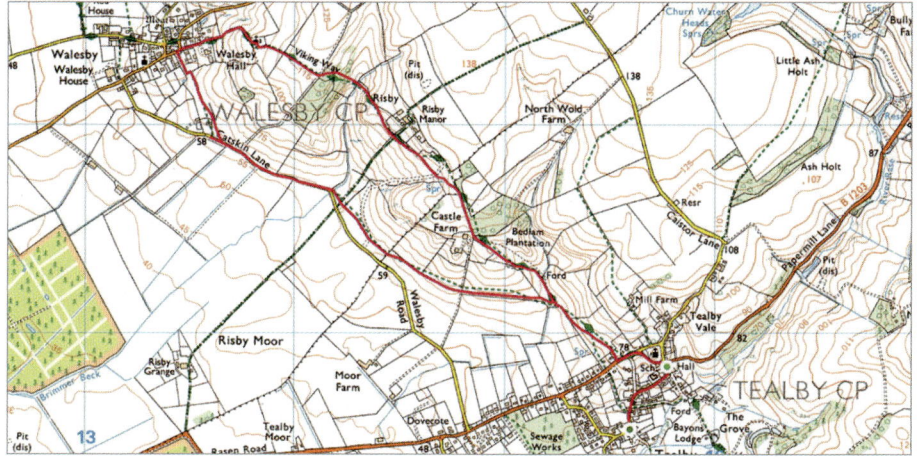

All Saints, otherwise known as The Ramblers Church, is mentioned in the Domesday Book and sits in a majestic position in one of the highest spots in Lincolnshire. There are great views across neighbouring farmland, and on a good day you can even spot the tops of the towers of Lincoln Cathedral some 32km (20 miles) away.

The church is reached by an often-muddy footpath from the village of Walesby, which you can now follow until you reach Rasen Road. Once you emerge onto the road, as it sweeps around a bend, continue straight on, and at a fingerpost follow the footpath to the left, across a field and down towards the small rural road of Catskin

THE PUB: The Kings Head, 11 Kingsway, Tealby, Market Rasen, Lincs LN8 3YA
🌐 www.thekingsheadtealby.co.uk
📞 01673 838347

START AND END POINT: Front Street, Tealby LN8 3XU

WALK LENGTH: 6.8km (4.2 miles)

ASCENT: 147m (482ft)

APPROX. TIME: 1 hour 45 minutes

PARKING: On-street parking available on Front Street (see above)

CAR FREE: Bus stops available at All Saints Church

Lane, which serves the village as a direct route from Tealby. When the lane bends round to the right, look for a little opening in the hedgerow and a fingerpost sign. Head left here, and immediately over a stile. You can then follow this route on the side of a hill back to where you left Tealby on the Viking Way.

Re-enter Tealby the way you left and head down Beck Hill, before continuing down Front Street with its well-tended-to cottages evoking a sense of quiet pastoral England. At the bottom of the hill, you'll reach The Kings Head, which is reputedly the oldest thatched pub in Lincolnshire and dates to 1367. Inside, you're enveloped by low-beamed ceilings, stone floors and a glimpse of the Wolds of yesteryear, with photographs and local memorabilia embellishing the walls. On a sunny day, the ample beer garden and well-kept lawn is a perfect place to while away an afternoon. Of course, Lincolnshire sausage and mash is the perfect accompaniment.

▼ The Kings Head is as traditional as they come.

25

LINCOLNSHIRE WOLDS & THE BLUE BELL INN

— 12.2km (7.6 miles) —

The Lincolnshire Wolds is a historic place, shaped by Romans, Vikings and early settlers, characterised by deep valleys and expansive views and crisscrossed by ancient pathways that have been trodden by its people for thousands of years.

The hills here rise from the flat surrounding landscape, creating a distinct natural boundary, and have influenced human settlement for millennia. The area's rich agricultural potential made it a hub of human activity since prehistoric times, and archaeological evidence (such as burial mounds and ancient trackways) suggests that the Wolds were inhabited as early as the Bronze Age. Following the collapse of Roman rule in Britain around the 5th century AD, the Lincolnshire Wolds, like much of eastern England, experienced a period of huge upheaval. The era saw the arrival of the Anglo-Saxons, followed by the Norsemen, more commonly known as Vikings, who left an indelible mark on the region. Many villages in the Wolds have names of Scandinavian origin, often ending in '-by' (meaning 'farm' or 'village') or '-thorpe' (meaning 'hamlet'). Names such as Ludford and Swaby are a direct link to the Norse settlers who established these communities during the 9th and 10th centuries.

▼ This walk takes you through classic, quiet and unspoilt Lincolnshire villages.

▲ The great expanses of Lincolnshire fields are home to a large proportion of England's food supply.

THE WALK

This walk weaves through a scattering of classic Lincolnshire countryside in between four main villages – Fulletby, Salmonby, Tetford and Belchford, where you'll find The Blue Bell Inn, a great stop-off point on this 12.2km (7.6 mile) stomp. There are a couple of steepish sections offering great views, but overall this is an achievable and enjoyable day out.

Park in the village of Fulletby, and head east towards the junction to the main road that runs south to north up to Belchford. There's a great view to be enjoyed straight ahead of you across the Wolds – turn left, followed by an immediate right-hand turn onto a path that takes you through a series of fields with a farm lane on your left. Fantastic views continue to open up in front of you and this walk is especially enjoyable in the early morning as you're facing east, so you can watch the sunrise over the surrounding countryside.

A patch of woodland on your right, called Salmonby Carr, is soon followed by the farming hamlet of Salmonby. The path crosses the edge of a small lake and emerges onto a lane, with a collection of large houses to your left and right. Continue left on this lane, and keep bearing round to the left, following signs to Fulletby and Belchford.

This lane ascends slightly and you'll soon have more far-reaching views. Keep going past some farm buildings, and before the lane curves to the right, take a footpath on your right heading once again into the countryside. It's a straight wander from here through a large field to another lane, and once you've reached this, turn right and then immediately left to follow the waymarked route into Tetford.

Tetford is a working place fringed with pretty cottages, but press on once you're here. Continue along West Road, passing the houses, before curving round to the left on White Gate. Keep persevering along the lane for a few hundred metres more, and when the road bends sharply to the right, keep going and join Platts Lane, a farming track streaking through open countryside.

You'll rarely need to deviate from this path from here to Belchford, and it's easy

> **THE PUB:** The Blue Bell Inn, 1 Main Rd, Belchford, Horncastle, Lincs LN9 6LQ
> www.bluebellbelchford.co.uk
> 01507 533602
>
> **START AND END POINT:** High Street, Fulletby, Horncastle, Lincs LN9 6JY
>
> **WALK LENGTH:** 12.2km (7.6 miles)
>
> **ASCENT:** 155m (509ft)
>
> **APPROX. TIME:** 2 hours 45 minutes
>
> **PARKING:** Lay-by parking near Top Holt by the entrance to the footpath near Fulletby village
>
> **CAR FREE:** Bus stops available in Tetford and Belchford

▲ The Blue Bell Inn is located on the Viking Way, and provides a great place to rest weary feet.

CENTRAL & NORTHERN

to follow, although the feeling of being alone in such wide-open countryside can, at times, feel somewhat unnerving. However, this is beautiful and productive, working land, with a patchwork of green, gold, brown and grey depending on the crop. It's both impressive and humbling to know that this part of the country, like the walks we've featured in neighbouring Cambridgeshire and Norfolk, grows a huge amount of the food we eat in England. There's little to punctuate the scenery other than the odd barn, hay bale or farm building.

Once past Glebe Farm Low Yard, you'll eventually emerge onto Lowfield Lane, at which point turn left and follow the road back into Belchford. Here you'll find the The Blue Bell, a jewel of a rural pub with a giant blue bell swinging from its pub sign. There's a homely charm and after a good proportion of your day stomping around the villages of the area, it's nice to rest your feet in a friendly pub, with tables outside to enjoy proper rural hearty fare. With over 20 per cent of England's food produced in Lincolnshire, there's also plenty to choose from on a packed menu brimming with regional produce.

Once you're done, head to the lane opposite the pub called Dams Lane, which eventually leads you to a farmhouse. From Dams Farm, join the footpath south again, through and around large open fields on the Viking Way. Soon, you'll reach the northern edge of a settlement, and then you're back in the heart of Fulletby, where you parked earlier.

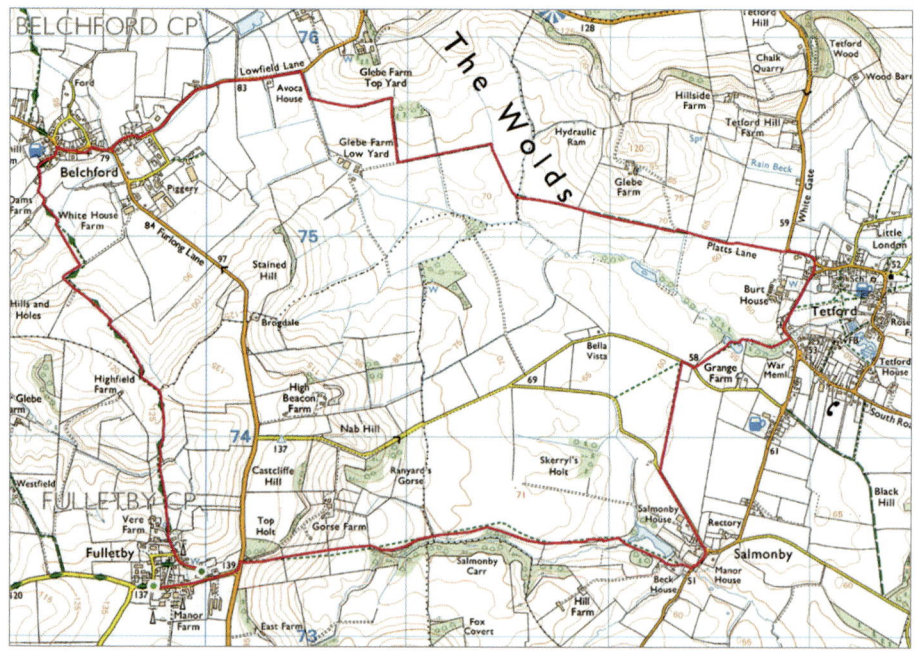

26

CAER CARADOC & THE ROYAL OAK

— 7.7km (4.8 miles) —

It's clear if you venture down any of the little lanes that surround the pretty village of Cardington, in the Shropshire Hills, that you're really in the depths of the countryside. Many of the lanes around here are little more than the width of a car, and as you trundle down them, you'll come across collections of small farming villages and hamlets that have sat untouched for centuries. To this day, they are still inhabited by people working the land; this is a rural county, and one that forms part of the Welsh Marches, flat in the northern areas and hilly in the south where the Shropshire National Landscape offers expansive views across the Midlands and Wales.

▼ It is said that Caer Caradoc was the site of Caratacus' last battle against the Roman Legions during the Roman conquest of Britain.

Like its neighbouring counties and much of the Welsh Marches, this is also historical, strategic land. The Shropshire Hills are steeped in stories, with prehistoric activity at sites like Caer Caradoc, an Iron Age or late Bronze Age settlement with advantageous views over the market town of Church Stretton and the surrounding area. The hill fort will be our destination for today's walk, and although it's a climb, it's a much gentler stroll from the village of Cardington and a less popular route than the path up from Church Stretton, so it's likely you'll have some of these lanes to yourself.

THE WALK

Start at the bottom of the lane in Cardington, on a flat piece of land used as the car park opposite the pub. As you pass the pub on the right, continue to head up along the main road through the village, passing St James' Church, which dates to the Norman period. At the top of the road, turn left at a Tudor house and, just past the house, immediately right at a turn signposted Willstone and Caradoc Hill.

About 0.8km (0.5 miles) along this

▼ Nestled in the pretty village of Cardington, the Royal Oak is a traditional pub that serves local farming villages.

▲ The walk offers great views across the large expanse of rural land in Shropshire.

quiet lane you'll reach a farm on your right, but continue to the left when the tarmac turns sharply right. You'll now be on an ancient track; an old drovers' road, which links the nearby markets at Church Stretton to farms and villages. It's not changed much here over the years, and it doesn't take a huge stretch of the imagination to picture these routes being used by ancient farmers to move and sell their livestock.

You'll now begin the ascent to Caer Caradoc, with views over to the hill fort ahead of you. Ignore the first two right turns and continue along the old drovers' road until you reach an information board about the area just past a gate. Turn right to begin your climb, bearing left up the slope, and you'll soon see Caradoc in front of you, the path curving left around the hill. At the top of the incline at a rocky outcrop, bear right and you'll reach the summit, with great views down towards the Shropshire countryside and the Long Mynd beyond the valley where Church Stretton sits.

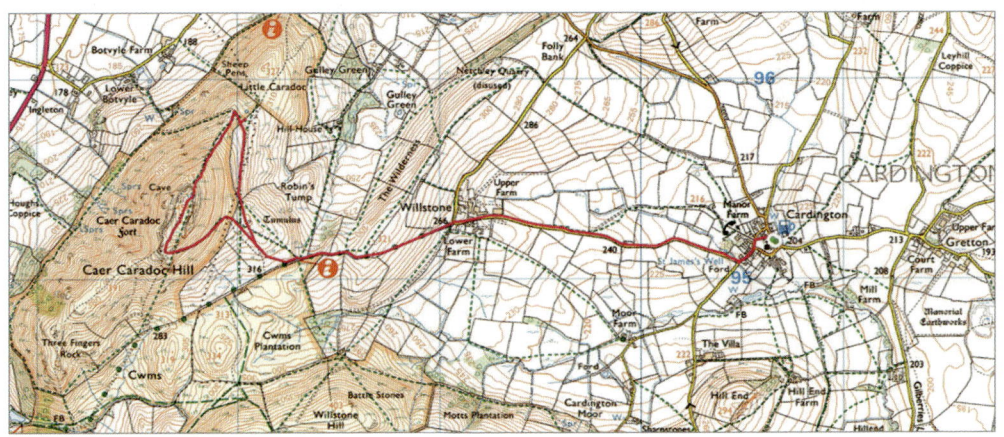

CENTRAL & NORTHERN

THE PUB: The Royal Oak, Cardington, Church Stretton, Shrops SY6 7JZ
🌐 www.at-the-oak.co.uk
📞 01694 771266

START AND END POINT: The Royal Oak (see above)

WALK LENGTH: 7.7km (4.8 miles)

ASCENT: 314m (1,030ft)

APPROX. TIME: 2 hours 15 minutes

PARKING: Car park opposite The Royal Oak (see above)

CAR FREE: Royal Oak bus stop in Cardington

cats sit nonchalantly by the fireplace, while I enjoy a freshly made Shropshire ploughman's lunch and a local ale. For busier times, there is a dining hall above the bar, but the whole place has a farmhouse living room appearance, keeping its sense of identity at the heart of a community that's easily overlooked by larger pub businesses. 'It's all the better for it – The Royal Oak is vital, especially when they're snowed in', says Eira, and it seems to me that no matter what, these are exactly the types of community spaces we should be visiting more and working hard to save.

From the summit, continue straight before turning right, and then immediately right again along the side of the hill to rejoin the path you started the ascent on. Once you reach the drovers' path, turn left and follow your steps back to the pub.

The Royal Oak offers a hearty farmhouse menu and local ales, to enjoy in the company of the pub's friendly animals who often sit by the expansive inglenook fireplace. The pub's landlady, Eira, offers a friendly welcome; 'It's so important to keep these small rural pubs thriving in this part of rural Shropshire,' she explains to me. 'So many local pubs haven't been able to make ends meet – we are at the centre of the community for so many people here.' She tells me this as the pub dogs busy themselves with their toys and the

▶ Eira, the landlady, explains how vital it is to keep pubs that service rural communities afloat.

CENTRAL & NORTHERN

27

BLACK HILL & THE BULL'S HEAD

— 10km (6.2 miles) —

The boundary between Wales and England is an enticing borderland, where tales of ancient conflicts and battles are embedded amid undulating hills, weathered walls and stone castles that bear the scars of medieval skirmishes. The landscape feels different here; the verdant greens of English farming land brush up against stark brown heathland, which hints of nearby Welsh mountains and peaks.

The Welsh Marches stretch between England and Wales and encompass primarily the counties of Hertfordshire and Shropshire. The term 'Welsh March' was originally used in the Middle Ages to denote the areas where Marcher lords had specific rights that were exercised independently of the king of England. To this day, the story of feuding lords and knights, of shifting allegiances and the ceaseless struggle for dominion, paint a vivid backdrop to the region's past.

▲ The Bull's Head's large beer garden is an ideal place to relax with a drink.

CENTRAL & NORTHERN

Winding rivers, like the Wye and the Severn, carve their paths through the countryside, and a patchwork of ancient woodlands sit in deep, hidden valleys. The borders here are imprecise and undefined, not just lines on a map but living, breathing entities, blurring the distinctions between two lands. In the villages, half-timbered houses, old farmyards and quiet, overgrown hedgerow-lined lanes dominate a rural scene. Even in the busy days of summer, it feels quiet here and somewhat romantic and sleepy. Craswall is one of those villages, not more than a few houses and dominated by The Bull's Head, the start and end point of this walk up Black Hill.

Black Hill is one of the most impressive peaks in the Black Mountains, and is also called the Cat's Back due to its resemblance to a hunched, sitting cat. Rising up to the west of Craswall, the southern part of the ridge leads to a rocky summit with views across both England and Wales.

THE WALK

A quick look at the map shows the vast number of paths you can take up to Black Hill, but starting at the pub car park, turn left with the car park behind you, and follow the path on the right up the bridleway a few yards further on. It's a sunken, and at times, muddy lane. At the top, turn left onto a footpath and continue to bear right at any junction, leaving farm paths behind you.

▼ Black Hill is a stunning Welsh walk with views across the Welsh Marches.

You will soon be passing a lane that leads to Upper House Farm on your left, but continue straight on here, eventually passing a gate that leads to the small Black Hill car park and the picnic spot. Here, turn right up the steep slope and keep straight, going up until you reach the Black Hill trig point. You can enjoy the views over Hertfordshire and the greater Black Mountain range here, before continuing until you reach a path into the valley below you.

Turn right at this downhill path – it feels like you're going back on yourself but persevere for about 1.6km (1 mile), until you reach the fence line. At this point, you're nearly at the gate you previously came through. Turn left and follow the route back to where you started.

The latest incarnation of The Bull's Head is the brainchild of Jake, Ed and Amie, who along with a shared desire to be closer to nature and where they grew up in the borders, started a regenerative farming enterprise that feeds the pub's

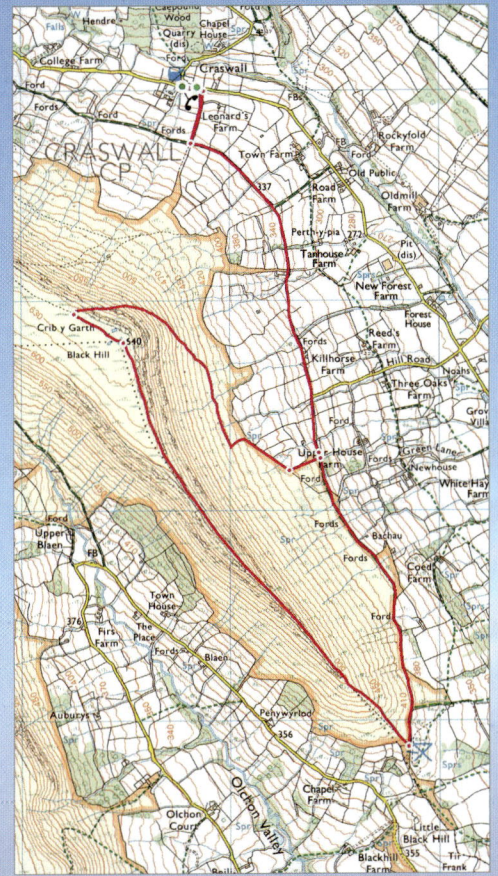

THE PUB: The Bull's Head, Hereford, Heref HR2 0PN

www.wildbynaturellp.com

01981 510616

START AND END POINT: The Bull's Head (see above)

WALK LENGTH: 10km (6.2 miles)

ASCENT: 392m (1,286ft)

APPROX. TIME: 2 hours 45 minutes

PARKING: Car park at The Bull's Head (see above)

CAR FREE: Bus stops available at Michaelchurch Turn

hole-in-the-wall bar and ancient flagstone floors. A small, cosy bar area is adjoined to a restaurant area and a large beer garden is the perfect place to rest achy feet after your walk.

Much like the surrounding villages here, there's a slow, carefree feel at the pub during the summer months and a warm, intimate atmosphere when many of the tourists have left the area. With little in the way of passing traffic, it feels really nestled in; protected and untouched by the surrounding landscape and, most importantly, by its owners, staff and locals, who are committed to running a business that's in keeping with the ethos of this part of the world. The Bull's Head is embedded in community and celebrates rural life with a passion. A visit here will certainly make you want to take a leaf or two out of their book.

kitchen. It started with some sheep, some cattle and a handful of pigs, and has since grown to include an on-farm butchery and a farmhouse retreat. The pub has been a landmark for centuries; an old drovers' inn with a traditional

▲ The cosy bar area in The Bull's Head.

CENTRAL & NORTHERN

▼ The Bull's Head is nestled within the surrounding landscape, and prides itself on a positive relationship with the local community and its surrounding land.

28

SLAD VALLEY & THE WOOLPACK INN

— 6.3km (3.9 miles) —

'This was the valley where I was born, and I knew every inch of it, every tree, every hedgerow, every pathway', wrote Laurie Lee of his childhood home. The Slad Valley, one of Stroud's five valleys, is a hidden enclave on the fringes of the Cotswolds. Its location within one of England's most famous national landscapes is, however, somewhat of a misnomer; this isn't the Cotswolds as we know it. Tucked away at the bottom of the valley's steep-sided hills, Slad doesn't adhere to modern conventions. Instead, it's a time capsule of rural England – 'a deep running cave still linked to its antic past', as the *Cider with Rosie* author described it. His book, *As I Walked Out One Midsummer Morning*, chronicles his departure from the village as a young man, but it's a place he returned to and loved all his life; the memories, stories and traditions he held so dear still evident for everyone to enjoy.

▼ The Woolpack sits at the heart of Slad, nestled within one of the five valleys of Stroud.

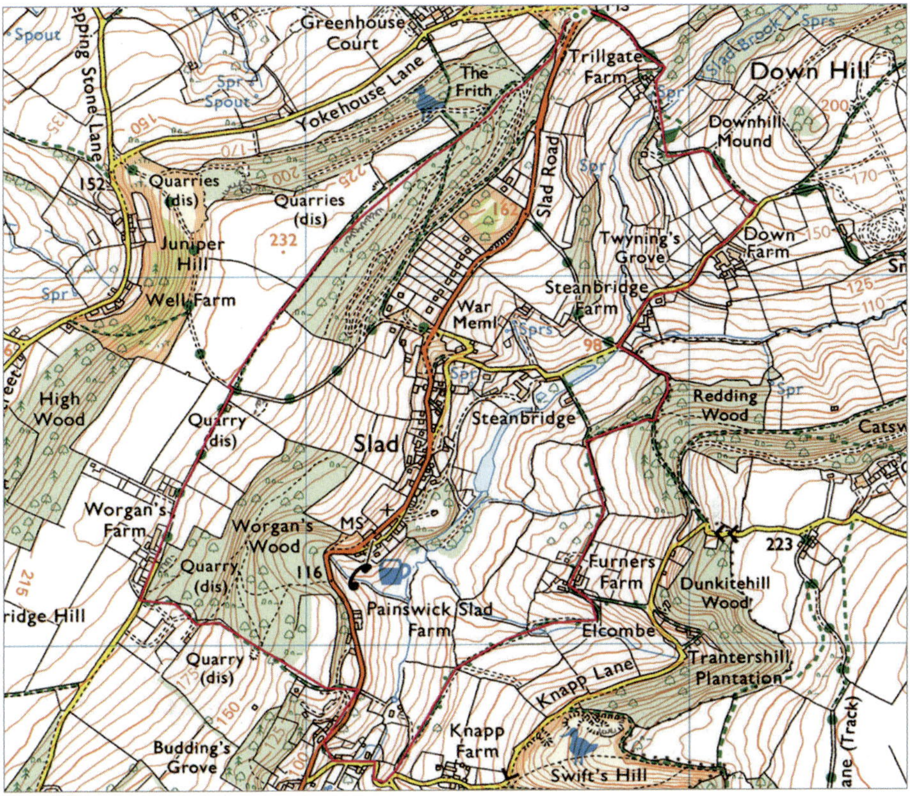

The Woolpack Inn sits at the heart of Slad. On a sunny weekend, it's not uncommon to see pubgoers, locals and visitors alike, spill out onto the street in front of the pub, gathered around a huge slab of wood hewn from a felled tree that acts as a large table outside. Inside, the old bar from Laurie Lee's time remains largely unchanged. To the right of the bar, a restaurant offers an excellent menu in a rustic setting, with views across the bucolic environment beyond.

THE WALK

For the walk, drive through the village of Slad initially and park at a lay-by just beyond the village, where Yokehouse Lane meets Slad Road. From here, just behind you, go down the lane to the right and wind past Trillgate Farm, with the expanse of *Cider with Rosie* countryside sprawling out in front of you. Climb to the top of the field that you will emerge into

CENTRAL & NORTHERN

▲ Laurie Lee's old home, Rose Cottage.

– at the right time of year this is awash with colour thanks to a smorgasbord of wildflowers. You'll rejoin a path that circles Down Hill, and then turn right on the lane, past the large buildings at Down Farm and on to Steanbridge Mill, a water-powered textile mill straight out of a scene from Laurie Lee's childhood memories of this area.

On the left here, there is a path that climbs steeply up a field (if there are cows in one field, you can avoid them by taking the other path) towards Redding Wood. Go through the wood, and if you've taken the first left turning, go through a small stile and immediately left through a field – there are great views here across to The Woolpack and Slad. You'll soon reach a small orchard on your right, before a clearing. After this, bear around to the left after the workshops and collection of farm buildings. Past Furners Farm the path divides, and here you'll take the right-hand slope downhill into the valley.

This is a magical part of the walk, and you're now deep in Laurie Lee land. Follow the path as it climbs to the top of fields, with old English apple trees dotting the landscape and waymarkers housing various pieces of Lee's writing relevant to the area. Go over a stile into the next field and then another at the end of this field, and left onto a small lane that brings you down to a road. Wind round to the right (spot the lovely badger illustrations on the fence posts), then turn right after a collection of houses, climbing through the undergrowth on a tiny path that brings you out onto the main Slad Road again. Turn right, and either head straight back into Slad and the pub, or alternatively, if you'd like to drive back to the pub, turn left through an opening that climbs up the other side of the valley a short way on from where you emerged (as mapped).

Once you've emerged through the trees and come out after a brisk climb onto a paved road, turn right and follow the lane, choosing to either turn right after a disused quarry to visit The Woolpack Inn, or continue straight on towards a patch of woodland known as The Frith, which leads straight back to the car.

This walk takes in a small part of the Laurie Lee landscape, and in the pub, you'll learn more about the writer and his stories of the people in this area. Lee's portrayal of the valley is not just a celebration of its beauty, but also a reflection on the passage of time. His writing captures a world on the cusp of transformation, as traditional rural life began to give way to modernity, but at The Woolpack, a small part of this old world remains. 'The Woolpack was the heart of the village, a place where people came together to share stories, laughter, and sometimes tears,' he writes.

Lee's deep affection for the valley and its people is clearly celebrated in the pub. It's best visited on an early evening on a sunny summer's day, when the village comes alive, the soundtrack of birdsong accompanies the dialogue of pubgoers, and the sun is setting over the valley. With a pint of local cider in hand, it's not hard to make time stand still, imagining the tapestry of rural life playing out in this unassuming valley across the generations.

> THE PUB: The Woolpack Inn, Slad Rd, Slad, Stroud, Glos GL6 7QA
> www.thewoolpackslad.com
> 01452 234290
>
> START AND END POINT: Bulls Cross, Stroud, Glos GL6 7QF
> WALK LENGTH: 6.3km (3.9 miles)
> ASCENT: 233m (764ft)
> APPROX. TIME: 1 hour 45 minutes
> PARKING: Lay-by at Bulls Cross (see above)
> CAR FREE: Bulls Cross bus stop for local services from Stroud and surrounding area

▼ The interior of The Woolpack is true to its roots and a warm, inviting place to spend a while. There's also a fantastic rustic restaurant area, plus plenty of outdoor seating.

29

FOTHERINGHAY, ELTON & THE FALCON INN

— 9km (5.6 miles) —

Very little remains of Fotheringhay. At least, not if you knew it in the High Middle Ages, when the royal inhabitants of the large motte and bailey castle here ruled much of Northamptonshire. Famous for being the birthplace of Richard III and the final execution site of Mary, Queen of Scots, it's now a nationally important scheduled monument and an archaeological site. For obvious reasons, what's left has been protected, but much of the castle was completely demolished in the mid-1600s, hiding beneath the surface the grandeur and drama that unfolded here. Situated right next to the River Nene, the castle is the starting point for this walk, just outside the village.

Fotheringhay itself is not a big place, but today it is dominated by St Mary & All Saints Church, which houses the mausoleum to leading members of the House of York. It's a huge, imposing building, looming over this flat landscape as a relic of the rulers of yesteryear.

THE WALK

You can park near the church – walk past it on your right and continue towards a pretty row of old thatched houses, continuing until the road bears sharply right. Stay ahead on a farm track here.

Go through a kissing gate to explore the ruins of the castle on the banks of the river, before continuing towards the Nene Way. This is a well-marked route, forking at the first right away from the farm track on which you left the village, past Castle Farm campsite and on towards a large field. You'll cross a dismantled railway line here before joining a track, passing through a gate and reaching a lock, at which point you'll cross the river.

The riverbanks here are green, lush and teeming with wildlife, and at this point, you cross a couple of footbridges to reach a marina next to a large main road. Turn left before you arrive at the subway under the road and follow the path parallel to it for a few minutes, before you reach the first opportunity to turn left. Do so, and cross into the Elton Park estate.

Follow the bridleway over a brook and past clumps of woodland before you reach some houses, signalling the

▲ Old thatch cottages line the main street through Fotheringhay.

◀ The view from what remains of the castle towards St Mary & All Saints Church.

THE PUB: The Falcon Inn, Fotheringhay, Peterborough, Northants PE8 5HZ
🌐 www.thefalcon-inn.co.uk
📞 01832 226254

START AND END POINT: St Mary & All Saints Church, Castle Mound, Fotheringhay, Northants PE8 5HZ

WALK LENGTH: 9km (5.6 miles)

ASCENT: 52m (171ft)

APPROX. TIME: 2 hours

PARKING: On-road parking in Fotheringhay

CAR FREE: Nearest bus stops in Elton

start of the village of Elton. Before the first house on your right, turn right and follow the field uphill towards the church. Join the connecting road and turn left, go past a school on your left and then turn left again at Middle Street.

Middle Street in Elton is a road of charming cottages with well-tended gardens bursting with blooms. It's a picturesque scene, with an amiable sense of grandeur. Walk the entire length of Middle Street, and at the end of the road, when you reach Stocks Green, turn left onto a footpath that leads to an old mill and a lock. Cross the river, turn immediately right after the lock, and then left across a field. Cross the dismantled Northampton and Peterborough Railway line again and carry on until you reach a road.

Cross the road and the stile opposite, and continue to Park Lodge, crossing the farmyard, following the right-of-way signs. Walk diagonally left through the next field, through a gap in the hedge and onto the next field, with a line of trees ahead of you. Turn left here, and you're now back on the Nene Way. You can follow this path, turning left past model cottages onto a small road and then left again back into the village of Fotheringhay.

As you walk through the village again, you'll soon reach The Falcon Inn on your right. The inn is renowned for its exceptional menu, which has garnered many a local award over the years, but it's also the centre of the village; a

▼ The banks of the river in high summer are full of grasses awash with wildlife.

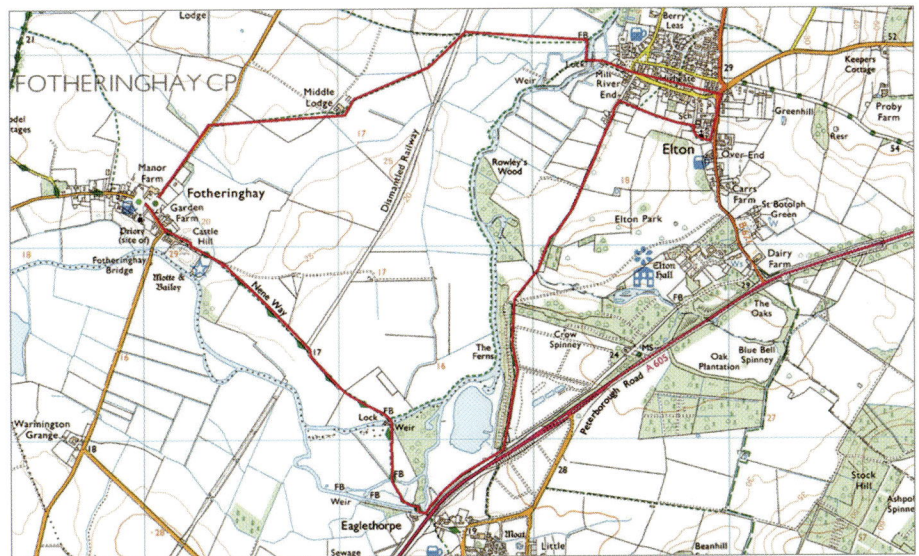

building not unlike the houses around it in shape and size, but with its pub sign swinging outside showcasing the village's links to royalty. It hosts a decent outdoor area and Madison and Zak, who run the pub, are rightly proud of their green ethos. Sustainability and environmental impact have always been at the heart of their offering, and in May 2023 they joined the Green Tourism Scheme. Excellent locally sourced produce is inevitable, from meat supplied by world-class butchers in Oundle, to fruit and vegetables from nearby Downham Market. They have a full list of suppliers on their website, and they also have an allotment where they grow as much as possible themselves.

► The Falcon Inn's pub sign hints at the area's royal links and historical importance.

CENTRAL & NORTHERN

30

AVEBURY, SILBURY HILL & THE RED LION

— 6.4km (4 miles) —

Everyone's heard of Stonehenge, but Britain's largest stone circle, Avebury, remains somewhat of a mystery. As one of the most significant prehistoric sites in Europe, it's believed to have been constructed about 4,500 years ago, around the same time as the Egyptians were building the pyramids.

Encompassing an area of about 11ha (28 acres), Avebury's construction lacks the intricate alignments with celestial events, unlike Stonehenge, but its scale and complexity are unparalleled. It includes three stone circles: a massive outer circle and two smaller inner circles. The outer circle originally consisted of about 100 standing stones, some of which weigh up to 40 tonnes and are believed to have been sourced locally, quarried from the surrounding Marlborough Downs. The inner circles, each containing a pair of concentric rings, were erected within the outer circle, their stones smaller. It's worth carrying an aerial map with you when you visit, as the surrounding National Trust village somewhat masks the location and identity of each stone, since it's nearly 10 times the diameter of its better-known cousin up the road. The Red Lion pub, in the village, serves as a fantastic point to start and end this walk, and it's one of a handful of National Trust-owned pubs across the country. It gets busy in tourist season, so it's worth booking in advance.

▶ The Red Lion pub sits at the heart of the village, surrounded by these magical and mysterious stones.

THE WALK

Park at the National Trust Car Park, cross the road and walk in a southerly direction towards the signage for the path along the river. To the south-west, a green conical shape rises in the distance – this is Silbury Hill, said to be the largest artificial earthwork in Europe, built in stages from as far back as 2500 BC. Nobody really knows what it was for, but it's been calculated that it could have taken over 500 men about 15 years to build. Excavations and tunnels have been bored into the hill over the years to learn more about its purpose, but only a handful of tools and other miscellaneous items have been found, deepening the sense of mystery.

Cross the busy A road once you reach it, keeping the hill on your right and following signs to the West Kennet Long Barrow. This is one of the largest long barrows in this area, and several chambers with more than 50 skeletons have been found here, dating from around 3500 BC. Nobody knows quite who was buried here, but it appears to be of huge importance to the area, while its sheer size and scale makes it one of the most important burial mounds anywhere in England. When you're finished at the barrow, double back on yourself until you reach a hedgerow along the path by the River Kennet.

Turn right at the hedgerow. This is a permissive footpath that you can take to reach the Stone Avenue, a processional route that would have been used as a sacred avenue to reach the Avebury stones. The avenue's alignment may have had astronomical or symbolic significance, guiding processions toward the sanctuary of the stones. It's believed

THE PUB: The Red Lion, High Street, Avebury, Marlborough, Wilts SN8 1RF
🌐 www.chefandbrewer.com/pubs/wiltshire/red-lion
☎ 01672 539 266

START AND END POINT: Avebury National Trust Car Park, 1 Beckhampton Rd, Beckhampton, Marlborough, Wilts SN8 1QT

WALK LENGTH: 6.4km (4 miles)

ASCENT: 76m (249ft)

APPROX. TIME: 1 hour 30 minutes

PARKING: Avebury National Trust Car Park (see above)

CAR FREE: Red Lion bus stop in Avebury village

to have been constructed during the late Neolithic period, around 2400 BC, making it contemporaneous with the later phases of Avebury's construction, and it likely played a key role in rituals and processions. It makes walking down here feel like you're literally walking in the footsteps of ancient Britons. There's a faintly haunting feeling, and as with many of these areas in southern England, the boundary between the present day and ancient history is constantly being blurred and reimagined.

Continue north through the avenue, until you reach the two portal stones that act as a boundary into the stone circle. Walk round the circle in a clockwise direction; the north-west

▲ Silbury Hill appears to have contained no burials, and its importance remains unknown as the largest artificial mound in Europe.

CENTRAL & NORTHERN

portion is perhaps the most impressive, with its Swindon Stone. Weighing in at 65 tonnes, it's one of the stones that has never been toppled. As you move around, take note of the ditch that surrounds the stones and appreciate what a huge undertaking carving this out must have been, especially with primitive stone and flint tools. It's thought that the ditch would probably have been filled at one point with buildings, perhaps made from timber.

Circling back to the portal stones, join the road north and back to The Red Lion pub. There's ample seating outside to enjoy a pint or two of local ale, before heading west along the high street and the heart of the village, back to the car park from which you started.

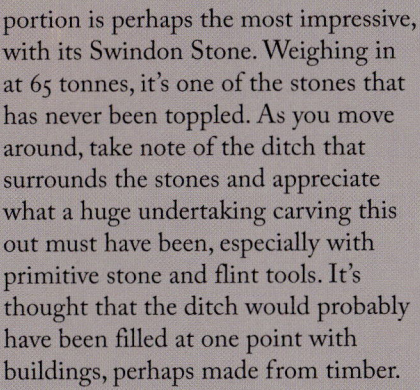

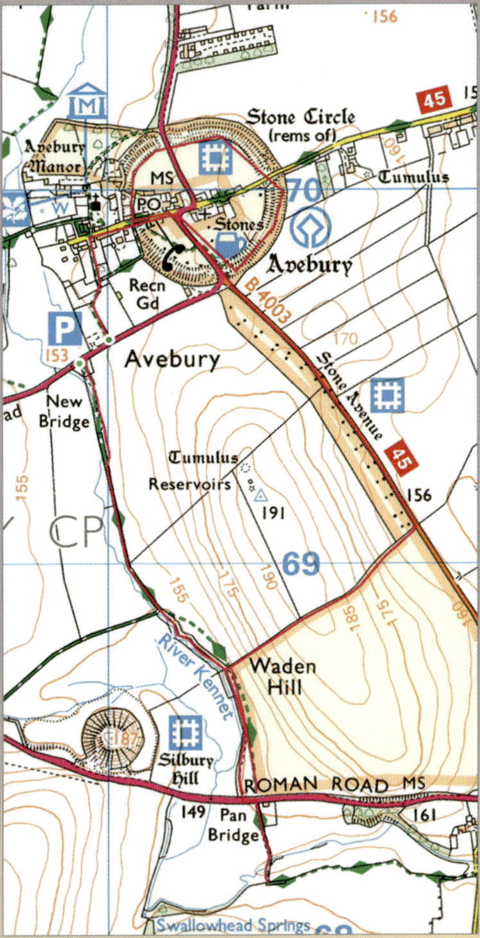

▼ The Avebury Stones at low light are an enchanting spectacle of ancient Britain.

SOUTH-WEST

From the rugged clifftops of Cornwall and Devon, to the rolling hills of Somerset, lies an ancient land of myth and legend. Celtic history, alongside echoes of industry and seafaring adventures, linger in the air in this storied landscape. Here, you'll find walks that take you from vast untamed inland expanses of wild moorland and countryside to the very outer edges of Coastal England.

The area was once a powerhouse of mining, quarrying, farming and fishing. During the 18th and 19th centuries, Cornwall's tin and copper mines were among the most productive in the world. These mines, burrowed deep beneath the Cornish rock, were vital to the region's economy and provided livelihoods for thousands of people. Today, walks like the St Agnes Beacon Circular offer tantalising glimpses into the remnants of this bygone era of toil. As you traverse this landscape, it's almost unfathomable to imagine how hard life must have been for those who worked in such unforgiving conditions.

From this hardship emerged a strong sense of community and resilience. Although now challenged by the pressures of tourism, this spirit continues to thrive. This is a proud land, rooted in values underpinning a long tradition of self-sufficiency and a deep, intimate relationship with both the countryside and sea. Through the 20th century, a

vibrant creative scene fostered a new relationship to the geography of the area, and towns like St Ives attracted artists, drawn to the region's stunning light and dramatic landscapes. The St Ives School, a group of modernist artists that emerged in the post-war era, helped put the town on the map as an artistic haven. You can see much of the land that inspired some of Britain's most famous painters in the Zennor Head walk, with a visit to the charming Tinners Arms (see page 186).

Further west, the dramatic cliffs near Porthcurno, sculpted by the relentless pounding of the sea, stand as guardians of the land. As you head east, the landscape softens into the gentler rolling hills of Devon and Somerset. Rich pastures, framed by dry stone walls and hedgerows, create a quintessential pastoral idyll. Pubs like The Acorn Inn in Dorset (see page 152), and The Packhorse near Bath (see page 148), sit as custodians of their rural communities. Nestled between the bucolic east and the rugged west, The Warren House Inn on Dartmoor (see page 160) offers its bleak isolation as the highest pub in southern England, and is the perfect base for a day of walking.

The south-west is vast and its coastline could provide years' worth of walking with its countless inlets. Inland, quieter, less-travelled paths lead to some of England's most charming small communities and provide an escape from the crowded tourist hotspots.

31

SOUTH STOKE CIRCULAR & THE PACKHORSE

— 3km (1.9 miles) —

Nestled within the rambling hills of the countryside in north-east Somerset sit countless small villages, their bucolic, old-world charm housing ancient stories of pastoral England. The villages and small towns in this area were once at the heart of a bustling rural industry, with the Somerset Coal Canal opening around 1800 and providing employment here, linking the large pits of the Somerset Coalfields to the Kennet & Avon Canal, and onwards east towards London and north to the ports of Bristol.

South Stoke is 3.2km (2 miles) south of Bath, on the route of the Coal Canal and designated a conservation area. It's easy to see why when you stroll through its main residential streets of historic limestone buildings, serene alleyways and historic churches with vistas beyond to great, green swathes of Somerset's gentle hillsides. Locals are quite rightly proud of their countryside, and The Packhorse pub website contains four different walking routes to download – my suggestion is route three which is detailed here and takes in elements of the impressive engineering of the Coal Canal and views across to villages that have barely changed in centuries.

THE WALK

Turn left out of The Packhorse car park, and left again past St James Church. Go over the stile and past the five-bar gate, continuing on with Manor Farm to your left as the path gently moves downhill, until you

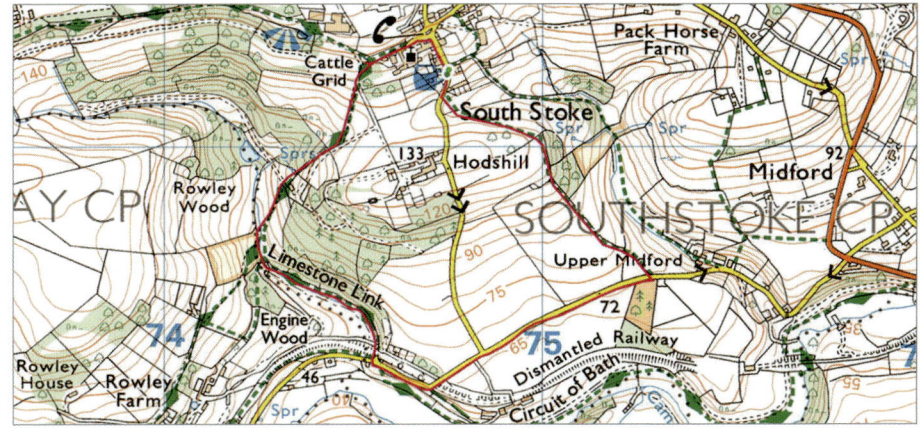

reach a large field. At this point, glance up; as you continue your downward trajectory through this gently sloping field the view opens up wide across the valley, and in the early summer it's worth taking a moment to appreciate the wildflowers. Purple orchids are especially impressive in June.

At the bottom of the field, you'll reach a patch of woodland, and past this is where the first signs of the industrial history of this area come into view. It'll become apparent that you are now walking on the canal towpath, where heavy industrial horses would pull narrowboats loaded with cargo from the coal fields at Radstock. It's 21km (13 miles) to the junction to the Kennet & Avon Canal, and then from there the payloads would continue on to the docks of Bristol or London to be distributed. Like in so many parts of England, it's fascinating to think that the raw materials supplied by the

▼ The small community of South Stoke coming into view at the end of the walk.

▲ During the winter, The Packhorse is especially popular and provides a cosy, welcoming space to spend an evening.

people in these small, remote, quiet communities drove busy infrastructure, heavy industry and big business in our nation's growing cities.

You'll know when you've reached the end of this part of the towpath because you'll reach a ladder stile – go over this and glance back to the view behind you. It's at this point that the canal's impressive engineering is apparent. Hidden in this valley, surrounded by a canopy of lush trees, you're reminded of how much of the British landscape is scattered with these memories of its rural history, long since reclaimed by nature and the seasonal routines of the British countryside. Most of it was built without any sort of mechanised labour.

Continue on along this path until you pass under a disused railway bridge, part of the line that used to connect Bristol with Radstock, making use of the sheer number of passengers that would have wanted to travel in this direction to work and live around the Coal Fields. It was closed to passenger traffic in the 1920s, and eventually, like many rail routes in rural England, succumbed to the Beeching cuts altogether in the 1960s.

Continue in a straight line with a grassy green field to your left, which used to be an area of the canal but was filled in with rubbish and waste from Bath during the course of the last century and grassed over. Pass through a gate, turn sharp left and continue walking up until you reach a road. It's a quiet road, and at the right time of year it's a great place to wander alongside the hedgerows. Keep going along here before taking the second left, up the steep slope known as Hodshill and down to the village of South Stoke once again.

The view ahead towards the village centre hasn't changed since the 1930s, and as you make the descent into the village, with wood smoke rising and its community tending to their allotments, you're reminded of the true beauty of the English countryside. From here, it's not long until you reach The Packhorse, the imposing building situated right at the heart of the village as you enter from neighbouring fields.

The 'Save The Packhorse' story has become something of a local legend. When the pub closed in 2012, it took with it its 150-year history and the stories housed within it. The following few years saw the new owners put in permission to turn the pub into a new residence with ground-floor office space, depriving the residents of South Stoke and the surrounding area of a pub to call home. So, a dedicated committee was formed to raise money to save the pub, and with other case studies of community pubs in the region providing a precedent, the money was raised and a buyout was negotiated in less than 100 days. A huge restoration project ensued, and the process is lovingly documented in a pamphlet available at the bar.

Through examination of the roof timbers, local historians have dated The Packhorse to 1618, and as a fitting end to the story, the renovation works were completed and the pub opened its doors again in 2018, exactly 400 years after its first days as an ale house. From the bar team to the locally produced art, the whole community's personality is within the pub, and inside, it feels like a truly dedicated effort; a passion project where a shared spirit welcomes newcomers, villagers and visitors with equally open

> **THE PUB:** The Packhorse, Old School Hill, South Stoke, Bath, Som BA2 7DU
> 🌐 www.packhorsebath.co.uk
> 📞 01225 830300
>
> **START AND END POINT:** The Packhorse Inn (see above)
>
> **WALK LENGTH:** 3km (1.9 miles)
>
> **ASCENT:** 106m (348ft)
>
> **APPROX. TIME:** 1 hour
>
> **PARKING:** The Packhorse Inn (see above)
>
> **CAR FREE:** Bus stops located on Midford Road – 12-minute walk from South Stoke

arms. With the fires roaring, it's also a wonderful place to warm up and recount adventures across this patch of Somerset.

▼ The large fireplace is at the heart of the bar area.

SOUTH-WEST

32

THE MELBURY PARK ESTATE & THE ACORN INN

— 7.4km (4.6 miles) —

'A traditional village pub full of life, laughter and good company' is how The Acorn Inn describes itself, and there is little argument. Tucked away in a corner of ancient Dorset, Evershot is literary country, and is mentioned in local writer Thomas Hardy's novels, while the pub is most notably referred to as the 'Sow and Acorn' in *Tess of the D'Urbervilles*.

This is a green and pleasant land, oozing with rustic charm thanks largely to the faded walls of this area's honey-coloured stone buildings. This walk is a circular stroll, taking in the grandeur of the Melbury Estate, eventually circling back round to respite in the pub.

THE WALK

There's parking available at The Acorn Inn and with the pub door behind you, turn left and follow the road past pretty houses. Ignoring the right-hand turn to Summer Lane, continue on and when the road bends round to the right, keep left and follow the paved driveway to Lion Lodge and the grand lion gates. Over a stile, the path then enters true British grand estate territory, and if you're lucky, you'll share your walk with a variety of species of native deer as well as grazing sheep and small collections of managed, farmed land.

Pass the turning to Lodge Farm on your left and continue towards the grand house. There's about 300ha (740 acres) of woodland, farm and grazing land here in the heart of southern England; testament to the latest in a

▼ The Acorn Inn is a rustic local pub, which serves as a great base to explore this part of Dorset, as well as offering accommodation and an excellent restaurant menu.

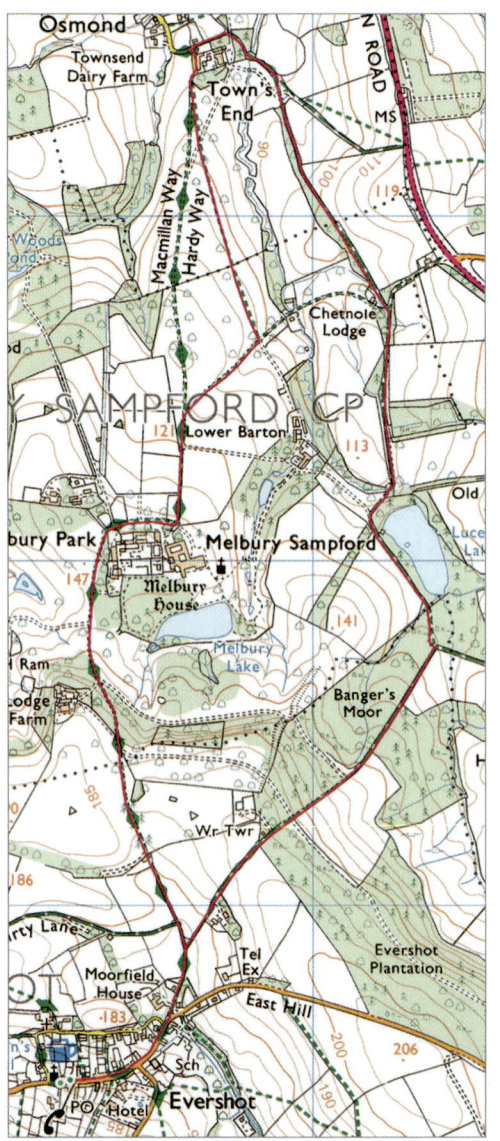

Melbury Osmond is magical Dorset and feels like a place that time almost forgot. You'll join the road at Town's End and pass a series of pretty thatched cottages before heading right on a bridleway between two houses that eventually splits in two. When it does, take the right-hand turning under a small stone bridge.

Go over the next small wooden bridge and walk uphill, going through the middle of three gates at the opposite end of the field you've just entered. The path continues south-south-east here, and you'll soon reach Chetnole Lodge, where you pass over a small paved road and into a small patch of woodland. Keep to the right here and through a gate, turn left to bend around the edge of Lucerne Lake, ignoring the turning on the right to Lower Barton. When the path forks on Banger's Moor, take the right-hand path uphill and through Evershot plantation. When you go down the other side, you'll reach the junction on the path you started out on. Turn left to get back to the village and the pub.

Dating to the 16th century, The Acorn is a Grade II listed building, and it exudes a timeless character; its ivy-clad walls

long line of Strangways, the family who own the house and much of the land in eastern Dorset. You'll pass the house on the right and then turn left, following the Hardy Way north towards the little village of Melbury Osmond.

and gentle stone facades made all the more inviting thanks to a generous choice of local food, wine and beer, including meat from the Jurassic Coast, freshly baked bread from the village bakery and vegetables grown in their own gardens. On a hot summer's day, it's as typical an English pub experience as you're likely to get and there's a lot on offer, with 10 rooms to stay in and a number of different archetypal activities available, from darts to tennis and croquet. It feels traditional but warm, comforting and homely, and is a gentle base to spend a few days enjoying this neatly buried slice of precious Dorset countryside.

THE PUB: The Acorn Inn, 28 Fore Street, Evershot, Dors DT2 0JW
🌐 www.acorn-inn.co.uk
📞 01935 83228

START AND END POINT: The Acorn Inn (see above)

WALK LENGTH: 7.4km (4.6 miles)

ASCENT: 160m (525ft)

APPROX. TIME: 1 hour 45 minutes

PARKING: The Acorn Inn (see above)

CAR FREE: Dorchester and Yeovil Stations nearby, 20-minute transfer (the pub can organise this for you)

▼ The Melbury Estate is fringed by patches of traditional English woodland.

33

WORTH MATRAVERS, WINSPIT QUARRY & THE SQUARE AND COMPASS

— 4.3km (2.7 miles) —

As a peninsula, the Isle of Purbeck, bordered by water on three sides, feels separate from the sloping countryside of the rest of Dorset. From 1974 to 2019, the isle formed the majority part of the local government district of Purbeck (which was named after it), and while it now lies within the Dorset unitary authority area, following the abolition of Purbeck, the character of this charming peninsula feels as unique as the rock on which it sits.

Going back to Roman times, Purbeck stone has played a vital role in the landscape of the region, both visually and economically, and the limestone beds on which the area lies form the basis of Purbeck Marble, a variety of the stone. Its polished surfaces, used to create columns, flooring and panels, can be seen in more or less every cathedral in the south of England. It has also found a more contemporary use; the numerous artists and sculptors who call Dorset their home use Purbeck Marble in their work.

The famous Square and Compass pub in Worth Matravers is the start and end point for this walk. The pub's benches are normally adorned with the multicoloured down jackets of climbers visiting the area to scale the nearby cliff faces. It's a unique watering hole that sits at the heart of an old-fashioned village steeped in rustic Dorset charm.

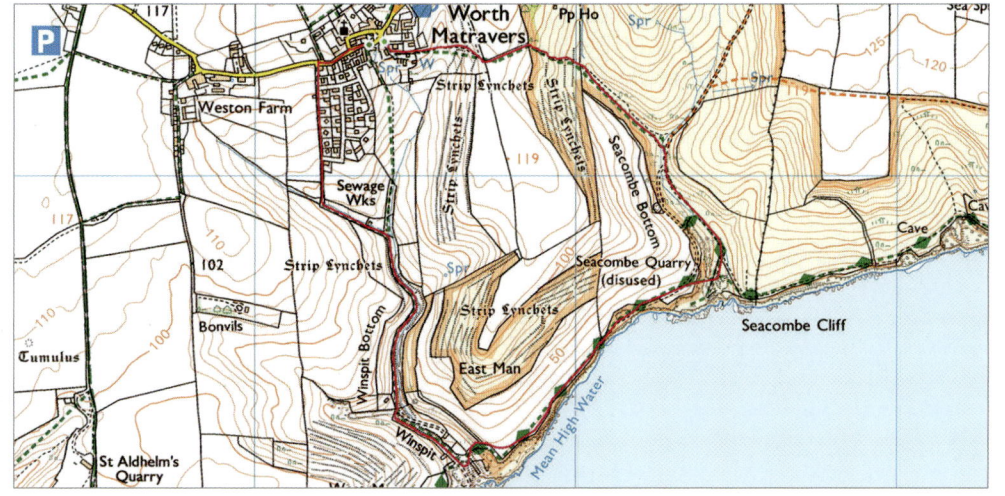

THE WALK

The Winspit Quarry circular walk is approximately 4.8km (3 miles) and offers a mix of coastal and rural walking. Start by strolling through the heart of the village, with a duck pond on your right. Next to the red phone box, turn left and follow a sign pointing to Seacombe, which leads you onto a raised path next to handful of small cottages and out onto a field. Continue across this field until you reach a stile and another signpost. Continue on again, keeping the field boundary on your left and the ancient strip lynchets below you on the right.

You'll now be going downhill towards the sea after passing a gate at the far end of the field you've just come from. Go down the steps, through another gate, and turn to the right. You'll now go across the stream and follow the clearly marked route down to the Seacombe Cliffs and the disused quarry. There may be a handful of climbers here – it's one of the quieter areas of Swanage in terms of climbing, but the scale of the rocks tell their own story. The landscape is in constant change, not just because of the historic quarrying but also due to erosion and permanent exposure to the ocean. The views here, both east and west, are majestic.

If you're on the clifftops, go back inland slightly and look for a stone sign that indicates where the coast path follows along to Winspit for another 1.3km (0.8 miles). Go through the gate and follow the steps up to the clifftop path. Here, the views are once again

◀ The dramatic Dorset coastline with clear evidence of the quarries that dominate the landscape's history.

SOUTH-WEST

157

THE PUB: The Square and Compass, Worth Matravers, Swanage, Dors BH19 3LF
🌐 www.squareandcompasspub.co.uk
📞 01929 439978

START AND END POINT: The Square and Compass (see above)

WALK LENGTH: 4.3km (2.7 miles)

ASCENT: 151m (495ft)

APPROX. TIME: 1 hour 20 minutes

PARKING: Worth Matravers Car Park, Swanage, Dors BH19 3LE

CAR FREE: Buses to Swanage from Wareham stop on Worth Lane, Kingston, or a 20-minute walk from Worth Matravers

impressive back towards Seacombe. Follow the path along the clifftop and it will be obvious when Winspit comes into view, its rock formations having a distinctly human-made feel to them due to the quarrying, with large, low, rocky outcrops signifying where the cliffs have been carved into. By now, you'll see colourful dots scattered across the faces of the rock, and on sunny days, expect to share this area with the many climbers who come from across Europe to ascend this famous bit of coastline.

In 2024, Winspit was closed temporarily for safety purposes due to erosion, and many of the caves have been closed off for bat conservation, but even just wandering along the cliff path and around these ancient formations alongside a scattering of old quarry

▼ With its grey-coloured stone, Worth Matravers is a unique spot in coastal Dorset.

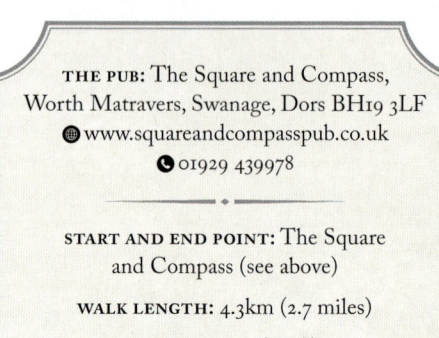

▲ The walk starts in the village across fields, but you'll soon find dramatic sea views.

buildings gives a haunting, otherworldly feel. The stone from here has journeyed all over the world, and most famously was used to rebuild much of London after the Great Fire in 1666. In fact, visit any building of significance in the capital and you're likely to find stone from this very quarry.

There's a clearly marked sign that leads to a dirt track away from Winspit. Follow this and it will lead you all the way back to the village – slightly uphill but easy-going thanks to its relatively firm surface. It's about 2km (1.25 miles) back to Worth Matravers, and at the fork in the path, either choose to cross the stile as a shortcut through the fields or continue along the dirt track.

Once you're back in the village, turn right and follow the road up to The Square and Compass. Established in the mid-18th century, it still has its original customer entrance. It doesn't have a bar, so head through the doors and queue at the charming hole in the wall, where a simple menu of local ales, pasties and pies await you. The simple bar menu

here is famous, and the expansive seating area outside, with its large stone benches and quarried tables from the local stoneyards, provides the opportunity to enjoy the simple and convivial atmosphere. Live music is served up regularly, with local artists playing on Sunday afternoons and many weekend evenings through the year. There's even a small fossil and stone museum here, the work of enthusiast fossil hunter Charlie Newman. It provides fascinating context to the landscape you've just walked through. On a sunny evening, with Dorset's glistening sunlight lowering, it's a quiet, simple and unpretentious spot, celebrated for its straightforward approach, and one that has stood the test of time for generations.

▼ The Square and Compass is a local institution, and also hosts a small but comprehensive fossil museum.

34

DARTMOOR & THE WARREN HOUSE INN

— 8km (5 miles) —

When you learn that the famous fire at Warren House Inn is said to have been burning since 1845, you get the idea of the welcome that'll greet you as you swing open the heavy wooden doors. Dartmoor can be an unforgiving, wild, atmospheric (and at times) scary place when the weather and conditions aren't on your side. The Warren House Inn boasts the claim of being southern England's highest, and at times what perhaps feels like its loneliest, pub.

Those in search of a proper moorland tramp won't be disappointed by this route. This circular walk feels wild, almost entirely on unsurfaced tracks with open dips and ruts in marsh and moorland, where unmatched swathes of wild flora play host to some of England's most biodiverse territories.

THE WALK

With the pub behind you, turn left on the road until you come to a small car park – take the path that leads downhill to the right. It continues down the valley, leaving The Warren House Inn a diminutive dot on the landscape above you. Large, open spaces of heather stretch out towards the valley floor and offer a superb view of the hills that rise above you on the other side of the valley. Here you'll find the historic Vitifer Tin Mine – expansive areas of this part of Dartmoor were excavated for tin, and many underground

► The Warren House Inn is the highest pub in southern England, and the only building for miles around.

workings here go deep below the moorland surface.

Turn right where there's a crossroads in the path at the mine. You'll know you've reached the right spot when you get to square outlines of stone; what used to be the mine buildings. Continue straight along the path towards the collection of trees with the Soussons Down plantation in front of you. Here, you'll find remains of the wonderfully named Golden Dagger Tin Mine, and you have a choice of routes. Keep to the right and you'll pass through some of the plantation, which was set up after the First World War and is one of the largest human-made coniferous forests in the area. Stay on this track and you'll reach Soussons Farm; take a left when you get here and continue on this track until you reach the outskirts of the medieval village of Challacombe, an abandoned hamlet that features the famous Dartmoor longhouses. Here, farmers and livestock would historically all live under one roof, and walking past them, it's a good reminder of how hard life must have been once upon a time in such a wild and remote place.

> **THE PUB:** Warren House Inn, Postbridge, Devon PL20 6TA
> 🌐 www.warrenhouseinn.co.uk/contact.html
> 📞 01822 880208
>
> **START AND END POINT:** Warren House Inn (see above)
>
> **WALK LENGTH:** 8km (5 miles)
>
> **ASCENT:** 225m (738ft)
>
> **APPROX. TIME:** 2 hours
>
> **PARKING:** Lay-by on road near the pub (see above)
>
> **CAR FREE:** 171 bus through Dartmoor from Newton Abbot stops outside the pub

At the organic Challacombe Farm, continue on what is now a fairly defined track north back up the valley towards another farm called Headland Warren. There are buildings here that were once said to be inns and other remote drinking establishments, set up for the miners who worked in the region; a cosy haven for weary workers toiling on the land.

Once you've reached this farm keep bearing to the left, with areas marked as hut circles on the map. You're on

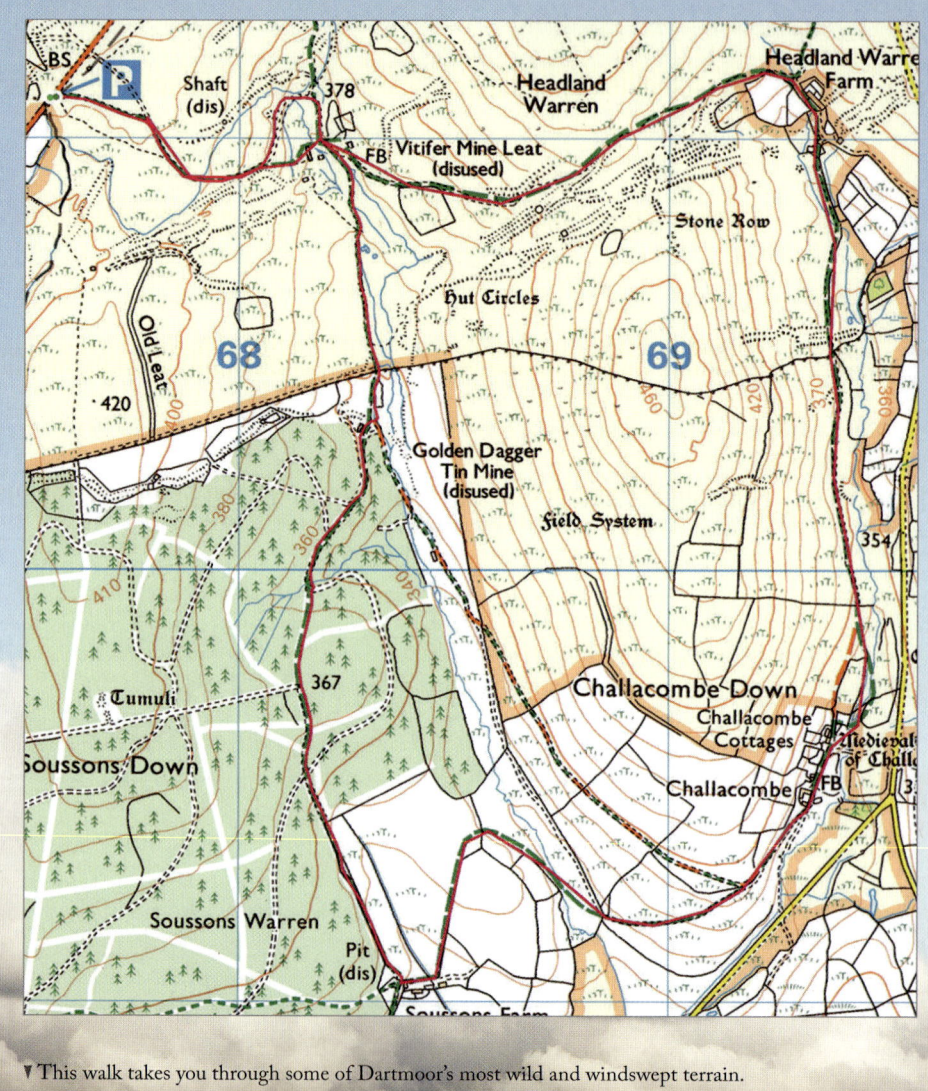

▼ This walk takes you through some of Dartmoor's most wild and windswept terrain.

▲ You'll no doubt spot some hardy Dartmoor Ponies on your walk. Written records of ponies on the moor go back as far as the 11th century.

the home straight now, and you'll soon meet up with the crossroads you went right at earlier. Keep ahead, and you'll be climbing back up the path you came down on from the road.

Keep heading up and you'll reach the road once again and the welcoming sight of The Warren House Inn. During summer, families play on the benches across the road and there's a busy trade of drinks and food service being plied, belying the unforgiving nature of the geography it sits in. The pub has no mains facilities whatsoever: electricity comes from two generators, and water is gravity-fed from a natural underground spring.

There has been a pub on this site since 1845, but the settlement dates back much further. Prior to 1845, there was a building on the opposite side of the road, which was named New House and provided welcome shelter for workers on the land. The name 'Warren House' comes from the plethora of rabbit warrens and, therefore, rabbit poaching

▲ The fire in the Warren House Inn has reportedly not gone out in centuries, and it's always a cosy and welcoming place to relax after a long stomp.

that took place in this area, supplying a large part of the miners' and farmers' diets during the majority of the 19th and 20th centuries. When the pub that exists today was built in the 1840s, the then landlord transferred the smouldering peat to the fire in the new building, and although wood is now used, legend has it that it hasn't gone out since.

Although busy during the summer months, you're not far away from being reminded of the isolated communities this pub serves, it being among the closest drinking establishments for the towns of Postbridge to the south and Moretonhampstead to the north, on the only road that stretches directly across the moorland. Scattered around the walls of the pub there are also more stark reminders of The Warren House Inn's remoteness, including pictures of the infamous winter of 1963, when the whole area was cut off by freak snowdrifts. For 12 weeks, supplies had to be flown in by helicopter, and as it's so high, it won't come as a surprise to most visitors that extreme weather continues to be one of the challenges of running a pub here. The fact that they manage it at all is impressive.

▼ A pint of local ale with one of the most stunning backdrops you'll find in southern England.

SOUTH-WEST

35

PRAWLE HEAD & PIGS NOSE INN

— 7km (4.4 miles) —

When dawn broke on the morning of 25 January 1936, the Finnish captain of one of the last and greatest sail-powered windjammers to grace the seas knew he was in trouble.

In thick fog, rough seas and worsening visibility, the *Herzogin Cecilie* had struck the Hamstone rocks off Prawle Head, near Salcombe, on the most southerly tip of Devon. The stricken vessel was a classic 'tall ship', a huge, four-masted, steel barque that journeyed the world's seas in the Australian Grain Races, the name given to the annual sailing season from South Australia's grain ports to Lizard Point in Cornwall. The *Herzogin* won eight of the races, and at the time was the fastest and most successful ship to sail from Australia to England. Dashed against the rocks on what was its last Grain Race, having travelled to Falmouth in just 86 days, the ship came to an end on the way to deposit its cargo in Ipswich. Everyone was rescued, and the wreck became a local tourist spot, until it was towed off the rocks. Soon after, it met its demise after being stuck on a sandy bank with concealed rocks just out to sea. It was a sorry end to a beautiful, majestic ocean liner.

This story is just one of the tales of maritime history that makes Prawle Head so famous. The area has held a long tradition of coastal defence and navigation, and during the Napoleonic Wars, it was used as a vantage point to monitor for French ships. Remnants of lookout posts and signal stations from various periods can still be found in the area.

▼ The south Devon coastline in the early evening sun.

THE WALK

This walk starts and ends in the small village of East Prawle. Park next to the green opposite Pigs Nose Inn, where we'll return to later, and leaving the grassy area on your left, head down the road curving to the right and down a small lane, past a no-through-road sign.

With a view over the hedgerows of the sea in front of you, continue down the lane and round to the left. Here you'll go past Little Holloway Camping; continue along this lane until it reaches another sharp left. The Prawle Head car park is down this road, so during the busy summer months, be mindful of potential passing traffic.

From the car park, you join the South West Coast Path and turn right towards Prawle Point, past a row of Coastguard cottages and eventually through a gate and onto the lookout station at the southerly most point of Devon. The fields around here were the site of a radar station during the Second World War, and there are grass-covered bunkers still evident, which now house a wide variety of wildlife species and diverse plant life – the National Trust owns this land and has been working with a local tenant to create a diverse, flower-rich pasture here.

▼ Gammon Head is a dramatic mix of coastline beauty and wildflower pastures to encourage a wide range of plant and animal life.

Prawle Point, from the old word *prahuille*, meaning 'lookout hill', was also the site of a medieval chapel. Now, the lookout is a National Coastwatch Institution site. From here, continue north along the path as it climbs through the stone walls of ancient fields. Follow the route as it heads over Elender Cove, with views out to Gammon Head.

At Gammon Head, rare plants and wildlife thrive, and as you continue along the coast path here, you'll reach Pigs Nose. Look to the left below you and you'll see Hamstone Cove and the Ham Stone, the site of the *Herzogin Cecilie* wreck. The undulating cliffs are rocky and dramatic, and as you reach a waymarker, you'll turn back inland, up a path and through a gate. Turn right and head uphill next, and with the wall on your left, go straight and you'll end near the cliffs again. Keeping heading uphill

THE PUB: Pigs Nose Inn, East Prawle, Kingsbridge, Devon TQ7 2BY
🌐 www.pigsnoseinn.co.uk
📞 01548 511209

START AND END POINT: Pigs Nose Inn (see above)

WALK LENGTH: 7km (4.4 miles)

ASCENT: 302m (991ft)

APPROX. TIME: 2 hours

PARKING: Limited parking around the Village Green, TQ7 2BY

CAR FREE: Buses to Salcombe, taxi to East Prawle

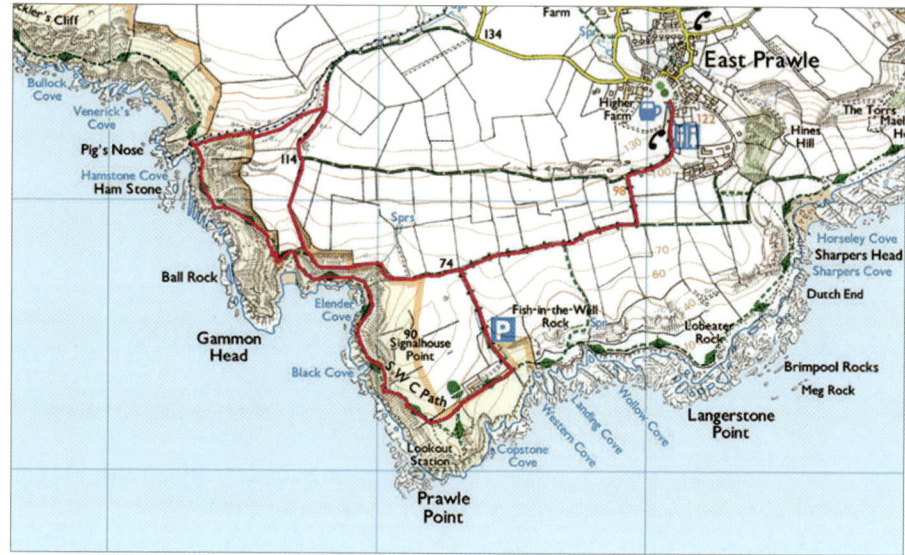

on the higher path, which eventually leads you to the road you were on. Follow this back to the village and head towards its centre and Pigs Nose Inn.

You'll meet a pleasing chaos as you walk through the lanterned porch of the inn. There's a faintly anarchic air, and with a longstanding tradition and a passion for live music, a good party is never far away. The inn is run by Peter Webber (an ex-roadie for big-name artists and bands), his wife, Lesley, and son, Joss, and it feels like the regular drinking establishment of many a musician from the halcyon days of disorder and mayhem. In fact, some major names in music have played here, attracted by its genuine attitude and the appeal of playing to small, appreciative audiences. The walls are agreeably cluttered with all manner of music memorabilia and charming tat.

With the prevalence of campsites in the area, it's a favourite late-night drinking spot for local canvas-dwellers, too, and the whole place has a carefree, laid-back and totally authentic atmosphere. For maximum impact, visiting on a gig night is an especially enjoyable experience.

◀ The Pigs Nose landlords have made the pub a haven for musicians over the years.

36

ST AGNES BEACON & THE DRIFTWOOD SPARS

— 10.5km (6.5 miles) —

The majority of what we know as St Agnes today was formed during the lucrative period of mining this area played host to in the 17th, 18th and 19th centuries. Tin and copper were abundant, and it's said that the 'ground is hollow' in much of these lands. Great lodes (a deposit of metal ore that embeds itself in a fracture of rock) stretch under farm fields, through the land's end and far out into the deep ocean around here, and these rich veins were mined for generations. The scars this industry marked on the landscape are easy to see on this circular walk in Cornwall's most prosperous mining land.

Today, St Agnes is a thriving north Cornish village. On any given day there will be a generous smattering of people going about their routines, and over the last decade there have been several lifestyle businesses, cafés and excellent restaurants set up here. The outdoor apparel and surfwear company Finisterre, for example, is based just down the road.

▼ The famous engine house at Wheal Coates mine, perched on the coast looking towards St Agnes Head.

THE WALK

Start on Trelawny Road at the St Agnes Village Car Park, and turn right at the entrance, away from the centre of the village. You'll come back up via the centre later, but for now, keep on this road and go past the Railway Inn. At the mini roundabout, turn right up Goonvrea Road and pass the village cemetery on your left as you continue to climb gently uphill.

At this point the road curves slightly round to the right. Take a signposted path on the right, called Cannonball Lane, and follow this route. When you reach a T-junction, turn right. You're now on Beacon Road, and the vista gets noticeably more unoccupied as you turn left between two farms up a dirt track, with excellent views down to the sea on your right and behind you.

The track begins the climb of St Agnes Beacon, and all the while the views of this area's coastline get ever more impressive as Perranporth, and then later Godrevy Lighthouse and St Ives Bay, come into view. Ignore the right turn as you ascend and pass the National Trust sign on your left. Go through the gate at the top of the hill here and bear left at the fork,

◀ Strolling out across St Agnes Beacon, the views soon open up to dramatic landscape vistas.

before hiking up to the top and admiring the view out to the wilds of the Atlantic. On a windy day, it's a thrilling, elemental place to sit a while. The Beacon's height of 192m (630ft), as well as its proximity to the coast, means that it was an excellent warning location. The mound you're stood on at the top is a Bronze Age cairn, and is anticipated to date from the period between 2000 and 1500 BC.

From the top, head towards the houses at the bottom of the Beacon. Take the right-hand fork when you have an option and continue downhill. Wind down and reach a farm track, where you'll turn right and then left on the lane, turning immediately right down a small, narrow footpath that can at times appear overgrown.

Having crossed the road and gone down this path, bear round to the right downhill on a small path. You'll reach a farm gate; turn right here to follow the path at the bottom of the field past some scrubland and old mining buildings. Keep along the valley bottom, over the stream you've been following, and turn right at the junction. You're now heading towards the small cove at Chapel Porth.

This area was the centre of the Charlotte United Copper Mine in the 19th century, and where the beach car park now stands would have once been a stamping mill, powered by the stream via a waterwheel. When you reach the access road to the beach, continue across up the coast path on the right-hand side of the valley as you look at the sea, and begin your journey back to St Agnes. At the clifftop, follow the left-hand path,

▲ The view stretching out westwards from the top of St Agnes Beacon.

which hugs the coast closest to the sea.

You'll now be walking through some of the most iconic landscapes of the area, with old mining ruins spread out across the cliffs. They're the remnants of parts of the Wheal Coates mining complex, the most renowned of these buildings being the Towanroath Engine House, perched sentry with little standing between it and the sea. It's worth making a couple of short diversions off the path to roam the mining ruins. The National Trust manage this landscape and there are a handful of information boards along the route. Past the engine house, climb up the old spoil heaps and continue to follow the clifftop round the headland, as the view of St Ives Bay disappears behind you.

On your right as you approach Trevaunance Cove, you'll pass a handful of capped mine shafts and quarries, before descending down into what was once a busy port shipping ore to South Wales. The elements have all but destroyed the harbours that were built here, but there's still an active ocean-going public using this area, launching kayaks, swimming and relaxing on benches outside The Driftwood Spars pub.

SOUTH-WEST

THE PUB: The Driftwood Spars, Trevaunance Cove, St Agnes, Cornw TR5 0RT

🌐 www.driftwoodspars.co.uk

📞 01872 552428

START AND END POINT: St Agnes Village Car Park, 33 Trelawny Rd, St Agnes, Cornw TR5 0TP

WALK LENGTH: 10.5km (6.5 miles)

ASCENT: 317m (1,040ft)

APPROX. TIME: 2 hours 40 minutes

PARKING: St Agnes Village Car Park (see above)

CAR FREE: Nearest bus stop outside the car park on Vicarage Road

---

The pub was built in the 1600s using 'spars' from wrecked ships – huge beams that now support the building. It's fascinating to see images and paintings from the associated shipwrecks through the years adorn the walls here, and the spirit of its sailors live on in the hundreds of pieces of rope, trinkets and memorabilia that can be seen around the bar. Initially, the building served as a warehouse for the mines, but over time it was transformed into a chandlery, a sail-making loft and even a fish cellar, before being converted into a pub and hotel in the early 1900s. There's a lively atmosphere here and the pub hosts a variety of events throughout the year, including its own beer festival. Freshly tapped beers from their own brewery across the road also means that a good pint isn't far away. There are also 15 rooms if you're interested in waking up to the sound of the ocean washing over the pebbles in the cove.

To finish the walk, continue from the cove up Quay Road, until you reach Town Hill. Once here, turn right at the small roundabout, past St Agnes Bakery and the bustling village centre, and back to the car park you started from.

▲ The Driftwood Spars at Trevaunance Cove enjoys an idyllic location and is a great spot to watch the coming and going of this community.

37

THE SERPENTINE CIRCULAR & THE CADGWITH COVE INN

— 6.8km (4.2 miles) —

The Lizard peninsula, at the southernmost tip of Cornwall, feels about as wild and windy as England gets. The ocean here shares these same traits, and the busy sea lanes around this part of the county were once known as the 'graveyard of ships'. It's a remote and ancient land, and a large area, flanked by only two major towns, Falmouth in the east and Helston to the west.

▼ The path from Cadgwith closely hugs the dramatic cliffs of southern Cornwall.

Interspersed among the rocky crags and inlets are historic settlements that exist from a bygone era; fishing villages and old mining communities perch on enormous clifftops that look out over seas of impending power and drama. Many of them, however, are also areas of great safety, and Cadgwith, a sheltered village nestled at the southern tip of the peninsula, has hosted a small fishing fleet and a hardy local community for centuries. The village is peppered with picture-perfect fishing cottages, their thatched roofs huddled together as if keeping close for warmth during the ferocious cycle of weather seen throughout the seasons in this part of Cornwall. It feels protected here, but the scene of a bucolic fishing community is only half the story. This is a real working village, with tons of lobster, shark, crab, mullet and mackerel caught every week. This walk showcases the best of the wild elements of the Lizard and passes through the prettiest parts of the village, with The Cadgwith Cove Inn, the natural community centre at its heart, providing welcome respite.

THE WALK

Start at the Cadgwith Car Park at the top of the village, and follow the sign into the centre of the village before turning almost immediately left and along to a stile, going back on yourself along a wooded ride. You'll bear round to woodland on the right at this point, before passing a gate, crossing a stream and ending up on the road to St Ruan.

You'll traverse the small village of Ruan Minor that sits above Cadgwith by turning left at the shop and post office, down a small track. Cross the road once you get to it, pass the school on the right

and the grounds of the Ruan Minor church. You're now heading into wilder lands and on to Poltesco, where there's a small car park and the impressive remains of a stone industry, that in the 19th century, once exported the instantly recognisable and eye-catching ornaments made from the local Serpentinite rock. This area is now managed and preserved by the National Trust.

Go through the gate at the end of the car park at Poltesco and bear around to the right, before turning left at a T-junction after passing a wooden bridge. Turn left again where the path branches, and you're now on the way into Cadgwith, enjoying impressive views of the craggy rock that makes this area famous as you pass Enys Head and its blowhole, which shoots a plume of water skywards when the tide's right. This is a cliff-edge path and can be treacherous in places, but is easy enough to manage with good, stable footwear.

As you enter Cadgwith you'll walk along a higher stretch of lane with views of the village below you. When you reach the bottom, you pass the pub on your right and the famous shingle beach on your left, where a small fleet of colourful fishing vessels stand guard. Choose to pop into the pub now, or continue through the village, up the hill on the other side and onto a surfaced

THE PUB: The Cadgwith Cove Inn, Cadgwith, Helston, Cornw TR12 7JX
🌐 www.cadgwithcoveinn.com
📞 01326 290513

START AND END POINT: Cadgwith Car Park, 2 Ledra Cl, Ruan Minor, Helston, Cornw TR12 7LD

WALK LENGTH: 6.8km (4.2 miles)

ASCENT: 239m (784ft)

APPROX. TIME: 2 hours

PARKING: Cadgwith Car Park (see above)

CAR FREE: Nearest bus stop is Glebe Place, Ruan Minor, Helston, Cornw TR12 7JW

◀ There is a working fishing community in Cadgwith.

▶ The Cadgwith Cove Inn is a treasure-trove of community portraits, and also hosts a vibrant local folk scene during the week.

SOUTH-WEST

path signposted 'Devil's Frying Pan'. This is a spectacular area of rock that was formed from the collapsed roof of a sea cave. In rough weather, the sight of the tide rushing into and breaking on what's left of the cave entrance is powerful. Keep on the cliff path here and enjoy the views, before turning right inland once you reach a stile and a small stream. Go left past the campsite, through Gwavas Farm once you reach a field and a sign for St Grada & Holy Cross Church. Stick to the left of the field, over a stile and past the St Ruan's Holy Well. Continue on to the road, which leads back to the car park.

At the end of the walk, with The Cadgwith Cove Inn waiting, enjoy views out to sea above the rooftops as you descend into the village. At any time of the year, there's a thriving feeling of locality and togetherness at the pub, which hosts folk jam sessions on Tuesday nights throughout the year and seafood barbecues during the summer months. Everyone plays a part in making these community events come to life, and you get the impression of the necessity of this. Tucked into a cosy corner with a fire lit, it's easy to forget that there's an unforgiving, wild Atlantic Ocean on the doorstep beyond the thick protective walls. Pictures of generations of fisherman and sailors adorn the walls, with letters, annotations and handwritten postcards instantly instilling a warm, friendly atmosphere as the guardians of this village from days gone by look down.

It feels fitting that a pub such as this should have a homemade 'catch of the day' dish. Lobster is available when caught and there's a focus on sustainable eating from the sea thanks to the village's active fishing fleet. On a good day of weather, it's easy to sit outside the pub with a local pint, watch the comings and goings of the community, and appreciate a way of living in Cornwall that's largely disappeared from elsewhere.

For more local history and community stories, a visit to www.cadgwith.com is well worth it.

38

LOGAN ROCK, PORTH CHAPEL, GWENNAP HEAD & THE LOGAN ROCK INN

— 5.6km (3.5 miles) —

If I was asked to pick one walk in south-west Cornwall that sums up this wild outpost, this would be it. Here, lie small communities and villages perched on dramatic clifftop edges, the landscape on their borders glinting in the sun thanks to white sand beaches and turquoise seas that hint at the paradisiacal land of the Scilly Isles beyond. Verdant countryside inland gives way to rugged coastal outcrops, the best bits of which are accessible via the South West Coast Path.

In the village of Treen, the sea is largely hidden from view, but the salty air gives it away. You'll find a small community here with a pub, a farm, a café and a campsite – one of the most westerly in the UK and certainly one of the sites closest to the sea.

▼ On the path from Treen down to the edge of the land, the first view of the sea hints at the dramatic coastline beyond.

THE WALK

Past The Logan Rock Inn on your right, the road bends to the left and you'll see Treen Car Park in front of you. Turn down a small lane to the right of the car park as you face it, following a sign to Treen Farm Campsite. The path widens out and becomes a farm lane, and as you turn sharp left at the campsite buildings, the sea comes into view; a great expanse of blue stretching out before you. Once you reach the South West Coast Path, you're greeted by excellent signage, so follow the arrow to Porthcurno and look left at Treen Cliff down to one of Cornwall's most stunning and most secluded beaches, Pedn Vounder. Beautiful sandbars and shallow lagoons are created here at low tide, and in recent years it has gained prominence thanks to the power of

▲ The paths are well signed around this walk.

social media. The steep descent to the beach is on your left, but continue winding down to Porthcurno, following the path, and before long the Minack Theatre will come into view, as well as the shining sands at the beach.

Porthcurno has a unique history of communication innovation. The first international telegraph cable was brought ashore here, connecting Britain

▼ Pedn Vounder beach is a picture-postcard view of coastal Cornwall, and well worth the rocky climb down to sample its turquoise waters.

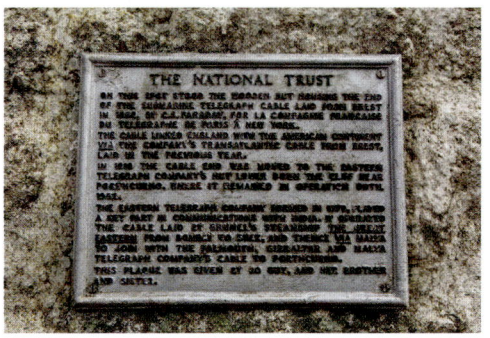
▲ Plaques mark the spot where the end of the submarine telegraph communication line to America came ashore.

▲ The red daymark on Gwennap Head acts as a reminder of the ferocious Runnel Stone a mile out to sea.

to parts of its empire over 150 years ago. Today, a white conical marker stands where one of those cables came ashore from the Americas – walk past this and wind down to the village, passing the PK Porthcurno Telegraph Museum on the way, which is a great place to learn more about this fascinating history.

As the route descends into Porthcurno, the coast path crosses the glowing sands of the beach, before rising up the other side of the valley and past the Minack Theatre, which clings to the cliffs, its stone seats perched waiting for the next performance under the open sky. The theatre was hand carved from the rock by its founder, architect Rowena Cade, who bought the Minack Headland in the early 1920s for £100. She built her home here, Minack House, and chipped away at the rocks with her gardener Billy Rawlings. It would take the rest of her life to build, and today it's an impressive setup, with local and national performances throughout the summer season.

As you continue along the coast path, you'll next reach the small fishing village of Porthgwarra, a handful of boats still using the steep granite slipway that was constructed in the mid-19th century. The tunnels you see carved into the rock were built to give local farmers easy access to the sea, where they collected seaweed for fertiliser. Continue up the other side of Porthgwarra and then on to the wild moorland landscape of Hella Point, following the coast path round to the daymark and lookout station at Gwennap Head.

The waters around Gwennap Head are some of the most infamous and treacherous anywhere in England, and the daymarks here are positioned to warn ships of the Runnel Stone reef, which lies 1.6km (1 mile) offshore. If the black and white marker is obscured by the red marker, it means ships passing this dangerous stretch of the channel are too close to the reef. Slightly further along the coast, there's a National Coastwatch Institution lookout station. Here, turn back inland and follow the track that leads to the buildings, turning right and back towards Porthgwarra on the lane that leads to the village. From here, turn left on the coast path and follow it back the way you came to the pub.

Dating back to at least the 16th century, there's a storied past to The Logan Rock Inn, which intertwines with the local maritime, mining and fishing histories of this remote, and at times ruthless part of rural Cornwall. Inside, it feels like a quintessential Cornish inn, constructed from local stone, featuring a thatched roof and offering a cosy, warm place to shelter from the outside world. Open fireplaces and a generously stocked, locally-sourced kitchen that celebrates both the land and sea adds to the warm welcome.

> **THE PUB:** The Logan Rock Inn, Treen, St Levan, Penzance, Cornw TR19 6LG
> 🌐 www.theloganrockinn.co.uk
> 📞 01736 810495
>
> **START AND END POINT:** The Logan Rock Inn (see above)
>
> **WALK LENGTH:** 5.6km (3.5 miles)
>
> **ASCENT:** 231m (758ft)
>
> **APPROX. TIME:** 1 hour 30 minutes
>
> **PARKING:** Car park at The Logan Rock Inn (see above), or Treen Car Park, Treen, Penzance, Cornw TR19 6LF
>
> **CAR FREE:** Nearest bus stop is Treen Hill (Land's End Cruiser Route)

▼ The Logan Rock Inn is nestled in the small community of Treen, perfectly placed to be enjoyed by walkers and visitors to the campsite.

39

ST MARTIN'S, ISLES OF SCILLY & THE SEVEN STONES INN

— 9.7km (6 miles)* —

Get ready to set sail. Off the Cornish coast, 45km (28 miles) west of Land's End, lies shallow seas, cobalt waters, white-sand beaches and a subtropical land otherwise the preserve of your wildest imagination.

Arriving on the Isles of Scilly feels like being transported to something akin to paradise, with five inhabited islands and over 140 uninhabited rocky outcrops creating a tapestry of spaces where wildlife thrives and the relative hustle and bustle of 'the mainland' seems a world away. Reaching the islands is an adventure in its own right, and part of the whole experience. Travel from Penzance on the Scillonian ferry, or fly on a tiny de Havilland Canada Twin Otter plane with Skybus from Land's End Airport at St Just. During the summer period, it's also possible to fly to the island from Newquay and Exeter airports.

THE WALK

Once you reach St Mary's, the island's only major hub of Hugh Town is where the action happens, and to get to this walk you'll first need to navigate the inter-island boats. These are colourful little wooden vessels, still made and maintained on the islands using traditional techniques and managed by island families for generations. Head to St Martin's, the third largest of the inhabited islands.

Get off the little ferry on New Quay,

---

*Taking into account the walk back to New Quay – shorter if boat departing from Lower Town.

▼ The calm waters around St Martin's on the Isles of Scilly.

at Higher Town Bay, and you'll be greeted by a horseshoe of crystal white sand and calm waters. You'll be heading right here on an easy path along the sandy 'road' that fringes a marram grass barrier to the beach and its pristine shoreline. Continue past St Martin's Vineyard on your left, a boutique winery run by ecologists who have a passion for sustainable agriculture and working in partnership with this unique landscape.

Pass the eastern edge of Higher Town Bay and the terrain will seem to get wilder. Look out to sea here and you'll see Chimney Rocks and beyond that the Eastern Isles, which are some of England's most special and protected sea rocks, a haven for seabirds and seal colonies. Continue on the path down to Brandy Point, following the route around and passing the St Martin's Daymark – one of the island's most recognisable features and the oldest surviving original daymark in the country – standing watch over these dangerous and wild shores.

From the daymark, take the path closest to the sea. The heather-lined coast now heads west and traverses ancient cairns, although the path stays obvious and easy to navigate. As you head up to Turfy Hill, the magical sight of Great Bay looms into view. If you haven't taken a dip yet, here's a perfect spot to cool off, the clear ocean providing a glimmering respite for weary feet.

The beach here is comprised of two bays, Great Bay and Little Bay. Past these, the route loops around the aptly named Top Rock Hill. This is the most northerly point of the inhabited Isles of Scilly. Look north out to sea here and

SOUTH-WEST

184

there's nothing but water until you reach the calm shores of Waterford in Ireland.

Back down off Top Rock and you'll follow the coast south with the islands of Tean and Tresco ahead of you. You'll be greeted by a calmer, gentler scene as you enter Lower Town and step inside the hidden, weathered walls of The Seven Stone Inn.

Here, you can sample the island's bounty on your plate. Like so many businesses on the Isles of Scilly, they are proudly family-run, and support a thriving local community that come together during the summer season to provide an exceptional visitor experience. Unlike some pubs on the islands, however, they do still open for a couple of nights during the 'off-season' (late autumn and winter). They even host their own gigs and offer a film festival in October. The pub is a vital source of commune for the island's generous scattering of permanent inhabitants.

Fresh, plump lobsters, locally-grown vegetables and island cattle make up the menu. There aren't many finer views in England than across the shallows between here and Tresco, and I always truly relax when stepping foot on these islands. With vistas stretching out across Crow Bar towards the distant northerly shores of St Mary's, you'll find yourself wishing you'd been forever shipwrecked on this most charming of lands.

When you're finished at the pub, either take the boat back from the quay on the western side of the island (depending on the tide), or walk back to New Quay. Check with the boat company in advance of your walk to find out which quay the boat is likely to be departing from later in the day.

> **THE PUB:** The Seven Stones Inn, Unnamed Rd, Lower Town, IOS TR25 0QW
> www.sevenstonesinn.com
> 01720 423777
>
> **START AND END POINT:** New Quay, St Martin's
>
> **WALK LENGTH:** 9.7km (6 miles) (taking into account the walk back to New Quay – shorter if boat departing from Lower Town)
>
> **ASCENT:** 311m (1,020ft)
>
> **APPROX. TIME:** 2 hours 30 minutes
>
> **PARKING:** N/A
>
> **CAR FREE:** Ferry from Penzance or Skybus from Land's End or Newquay, Cornwall. Inter-island boat from the main quay at St Mary's (morning and afternoon departures)
>
> www.islesofscilly-travel.co.uk
> 01736 334220

▼ From St Martin's, there are excellent views back across to Tresco and the other islands.

40

ZENNOR HEAD CIRCULAR & THE TINNERS ARMS

— 7.6km (4.7 miles) —

Drive west from St Ives across the northern fringes of Cornwall, and you'll soon be greeted by a patchwork of fields, hills and moorland that has changed very little for the centuries in which this dramatic landscape has been mined for its copious resources.

The B3306, more commonly known as the North Cornwall Coast Road, is consistently voted one of the most scenic roads in England. Cutting a line through ancient farmland, views emerge from behind rocky outcrops as the road twists and turns around every clifftop crevice. The place names along this road – Morvah, Bojewyan, Kenidjack, Bosavern – suggest a different world and hark back to this area's deep connection to its landscape and the Celtic influence that very much lives on in this often mysterious and, despite the tourism, relatively untouched part of the world.

▼ Walking out towards the tip of north Cornwall offers expansive views both east and west along the county's craggy cliffs.

One of the first settlements you come to on this road, and one of the biggest communities in the area, is Zennor. Viewed from above, St Senara's Church looks over the small collection of farm buildings and the pub, as was once the grip of religion in such disparate, fragile places. Situated at the heart of the community, it has only the Atlantic Ocean for a neighbour. It's believed there has been a small church here since the 6th century, and many people visit the area now to trace the origins of the Mermaid of Zennor story. Within the church stands the Mermaid Chair, a 500-year-old medieval bench end linked to the famous legend. It's said that a beautiful woman used to visit the church to listen to chorister Matthew Trewella. Disguising her mermaid form and hiding the fact that she was Morveren, daughter of Llyr, Celtic King of the Sea, she eventually told Matthew, who had fallen in love with her, that she would have to leave. Unable to live without her, Matthew followed her to Pendour Cove and was lured into the crashing waves. It's said that on still nights at the cove, you can still hear Matthew singing his love for Morveren from under the ocean.

The history of the community of Zennor reveals a dramatic cross-section of society through the ages. At the start of this walk, wander through the churchyard and notice the array of farming and fishing family names all buried here, alongside figures such as the artist and critic Patrick Heron and painter Bryan Wynter, who, alongside other members of the St Ives' artist movement, helped put this small area of Cornwall on the global arts map.

THE WALK

At the back of the church, take the path with the coastline on your left and facing east towards St Ives. This walk starts through the area's famous farmland and emerges halfway through onto the dramatic cliffs at Zennor Head. It can be rocky here at times, so if you'd like to get the difficult bit out of the way first, the route is also equally popular and impressive in reverse.

You'll soon be out of the settlement of Zennor and walking towards the area's copious farms, and surrounded by land for growing, it's not hard to see that this landscape has changed very little for many Cornish generations. As you progress through a patchwork of ancient fields and Cornish hedgerow boundaries, you'll come to Tremedda Farm, home of the Moomaid of Zennor Ice Cream and Zennor Wild florists,

THE PUB: The Tinners Arms, Zennor, St Ives, Cornw TR26 3BY
www.tinnersarms.com
01736 796927

START AND END POINT: Zennor Car Park, Zennor, St Ives, Cornw TR26 3DA

WALK LENGTH: 7.6km (4.7 miles)

ASCENT: 215m (705ft)

APPROX. TIME: 2 hours

PARKING: Zennor Car Park (see above)

CAR FREE: Buses from Penzance and St Ives stop at Zennor Turn, by the church

two unique local businesses set up by Zennor inhabitants.

Next to this is Tregerthen, which is owned by the National Trust and was home to DH Lawrence during the First World War. Continue straight along the path here, through diminutive fields and isolated farm communities with equally enthralling names such as Wicca and Boscubben. At Boscubben, turn left,

bearing towards the sea. Treveal Mill is in front of you – a Grade II listed building that dates to at least the 17th century. At the mill, go left and follow a marked footpath to the mouth of a wooded valley and a small stream that eventually leads to River Cove.

Once you see a sign for the South West Coast Path, turn left, starting to go back on yourself as you navigate the rocky outcrops and undulating twists and turns of the craggy coastline. Just out to sea, you'll spot the outcrop of The Carracks, home to one of the largest grey seal populations in the area (and otherwise known as Seal Island for obvious reasons). On a windy day, breathe in the air here. With seabirds and gulls whistling around the clifftops, and the salty spray from the ocean hardening on your lips, it's one of the places in the world I feel most at home.

As you continue back west, the view keeps getting better. It's said that DH Lawrence used to swim in Wicca Pool, and as you continue towards Zennor

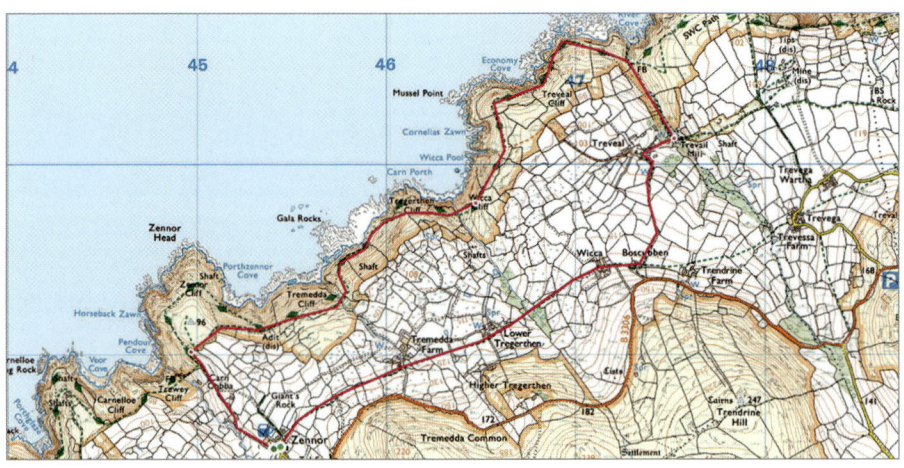

▲ The garden at The Tinners Arms, with the church in full view, is a great place to spend a summer's day.

Head, the highest 'point' on this walk, peer down towards Pendour Cove, where it's said that Matthew Trewhella was lured to his death. Look south and you'll see Zennor Hill, where local granite was quarried to build many of St Ives's famous fishing cottages. At this point, beyond the outcrops, you'll notice an obvious route back into Zennor, past a number of houses with large windows looking seawards, including the old Coastguard's house and lookout. It's not hard to imagine why many St Ives artists flocked Zennor-wards to set up camp here.

Inside The Tinners Arms you'll be welcomed with a roaring fire, low ceilings, a vibrant sense of bustle and a busy kitchen that hosts an extensive pub menu. It's just the way it always has been here – taller visitors beware: you'll be ducking to reach the bar. Granite walls, flagstone floors and a back dining room have a cosy farm feel, but there's a sense of artistry here with a creative undertone; it is, after all, an artist's favourite, and the local folk night draws crowds from across the scattered communities in the area. Nestled in a corner, pint in hand, with the windswept Cornish coast rumbling through the pub's bones, there aren't many more atmospheric, romantic or compelling places to get under the skin of a Cornwall that's fast disappearing.

► The pub sign at The Tinners Arms hints at this area's history.

SOUTH-EAST

Although south-east England is often overshadowed by its capital, London, it would be a mistake to think that the entire area has been subsumed by the city. The south-east is England's historic gateway to the country, shaped by centuries of migration, trade and conquest, alongside its proximity to Europe and the sea. From the white cliffs of Dover and the rolling hills of the South Downs, to the medieval streets of Canterbury and the flat expanse of Suffolk and Norfolk, the south-east tells the story of England's rich and complex history – from kings and queens, industrial power and thriving communities, all embedded within a picture-book of Englishness.

Geographically, the South Downs, stretching from Hampshire to the cliffs of East Sussex, are perhaps the most iconic natural feature of the region. These chalk hills offer stunning views across the English Channel and the surrounding countryside. Walks such as Firle Beacon (see page 217) and Beachy Head (see page 221) allow visitors to fully appreciate the beauty of this landscape. Further east, the Kent Downs and walks near Rye (see page 226), offer a glimpse into the grandeur of England's past and its role as a key trading post for Europe.

The south-east is also dotted with ancient settlements, royal palaces and cathedrals. In the Anglo-Saxon

period, the region was home to several powerful kingdoms, and the Norman conquest of 1066 left a lasting mark. Many castles were built during this time to secure Norman control, and numerous fortifications still stand today, a reminder of the area's strategic importance throughout history.

As the centuries wore on and industry developed, towns like Lewes and Guildford became hubs for wool production, and the fertile land of Suffolk, Norfolk and Cambridgeshire continue to offer much of the country's farming land. As the Industrial Revolution took hold, construction of the railways played a critical role in the region's growth, transforming both the economy and the way of life by making travel easier and spurring the development of suburban communities.

Prosperity flourished in these areas, and today parts of the south-east are among the wealthiest in the country, and home to some of the most affluent people in the world. Walks around Hambleden and Shere provide some insight into a bygone era, where rural life was steeped in English charm, untouched by the sprawl of London. I hope that many of the walks chosen in the south-east evoke that sense of stepping back in time, despite their proximity to one of the world's most forward-thinking and dynamic cities.

41

HELHOUGHTON, RAYNHAM & SCULTHORPE MILL

— 16.6km (10.3 miles) —

With enormous wide-open skies, huge fields that belong to England's rich farming tradition and a climate that feels more akin to Continental Europe during the summer months, you'd be forgiven for thinking this area of Norfolk is cut from a different cloth than other areas of the south-east. Inland, away from the coast, you'll find a land of babbling rivers, whispering willows that gracefully meet the water's edge and collections of quiet rural villages and communities that give the area a feeling of a hidden England; protected, sheltered and enshrined in a communal desire not to spoil the best of what they already have.

North Norfolk is well known for its scenic coastal beauty and holiday spots, but head further south near the market town of Fakenham and you'll find an entirely different scene. Long, winding lanes that end in nowhere but small churches and villages that back onto enormous estates – old money is the name of the game here – the landed gentry in Norfolk contributing to this day a large proportion of the county's atmosphere. This is where the top echelons of the upper class spend their time. Not far away from Sandringham and close to Raynham Hall, the seat of the Townshend family, large estates and houses dominate the landscape, offering views of expansive gardens and parklands. These estates were pivotal in advancing agricultural techniques and innovations, such as crop rotation and selective breeding, while the enclosure movement transformed Norfolk's rural economy. The county became a model of agricultural efficiency, and is often referred to as the 'breadbasket of Britain'.

THE WALK

Sculthorpe Mill is a large building situated on the River Wensum. The mill itself, an enchanting 18th-century building, is cradled by the gentle bends of the river, a designated Site of Special Scientific Interest, which flows gracefully beneath the pub. The riverbanks here are a haven for wildlife, with kingfishers darting in vibrant flashes of blue and otters slipping through the water. In the spring and summer months, the air is alive with the hum of dragonflies.

Historically, Norfolk's prosperity has been intertwined with its waterways. The River Wensum, once vital for trade and transport, saw countless mills and wharves spring up along its banks. Sculthorpe Mill was one such mill, grinding grain for the local community and playing a crucial role in the agrarian economy. Today, it stands as a beautifully restored relic of the past, owned by Siobhan and Caitriona Peyton, sisters of Oliver Peyton, the celebrated restaurant critic. As you'd imagine, the food is excellent here; but so are the surroundings – the pub has a generous, smartly decorated restaurant and bar area but also a fantastic garden, well-planted in a cottage style. It's a very pleasant place to sit and enjoy a sunny afternoon.

For the walk, you can either drive and park outside the church at Helhoughton, or alternatively, for a real taste of the quieter parts of the county, start at the pub and turn right, following the bend of the little lane with the pub on your right.

Keep going along this road until you reach a junction with a white fingerpost sign; turn right here, towards the collection of houses and into the hamlet

▼ The garden at the Sculthorpe Mill sits at the heart of the pub, and its expansive green area provides the perfect environment for lazy summer days.

of Shereford, bearing around to the left at the church. The lane continues and climbs steadily uphill, with views out to the right across Shereford Common. Take the left at the fork and continue along this road, passing farm buildings and enjoying the great expanse of Norfolk's huge sky. You'll soon reach a T-junction with a larger road – turn right here, following the route into Helhoughton.

At Helhoughton, take a path down to the left just before the church, with pretty cottages lining the lane. Keep bearing left and you'll reach a plantation, with a giant lake that was created when the River Wensum was dammed to create a 'pond' for the great Raynham Hall. Follow the path around past the Dutch-style barns at Stableyard Farm and soon St Mary's Church will come into view. Past the church, when the lane reaches the road, turn left and immediately left again, skirting the edge of a field towards the village of East Raynham, with the Great Hall to your left.

You'll emerge onto the A1065 – this is a busy road, but turn right here and follow the pavement past turnings to Lodge Farm and meadow camping sites until you reach a large, square, brick house and a turning on your right. Take this turn away from the busy road and then immediately left following the footpath sign through the field. Through into the next field, take the right path, which leads you north back up to the village of West Raynham and the remains of St Margaret's Church, which was abandoned in the 18th century. Continue through the village and bear right past the play area, following the lane past a cemetery and back to Helhoughton.

From Helhoughton, turn right, past the impressive church on your left, taking a small path through a field, which then joins up to the road you entered the village on earlier. From here, you can retrace your steps exactly back to the Sculthorpe Mill pub for a well-earned pint of Norfolk's famous local bitter.

> **THE PUB:** Sculthorpe Mill, Lynn Road, Sculthorpe, Fakenham, Norf NR21 9QG
> 🌐 www.sculthorpemill.uk
> 📞 01328 633001
>
> **START AND END POINT:** Sculthorpe Mill (see above)
>
> **WALK LENGTH:** 16.6km (10.3 miles)
>
> **ASCENT:** 114m (374ft)
>
> **APPROX. TIME:** 3 hours 45 minutes
>
> **PARKING:** Sculthorpe Mill (see above)
>
> **CAR FREE:** Bus stops near Sculthorpe Village Hall, north of the A148

▲ The church at Helhoughton.

SOUTH-EAST

42

PIN MILL, RIVER ORWELL CIRCULAR & THE BUTT & OYSTER

— 4.8km (3 miles) —

During the 19th and early 20th centuries, if you lived anywhere in England's capital, it's likely that the red sails of the Thames sailing barge were a common sight. These flat-bottomed, wooden-hulled boats were used for many decades to transport cargo, building materials and supplies into London. When the city was a trading centre for cargo from across the world, these barges often made the final journey into London since they were well-suited to the silty Thames Estuary, with its shallow waters and narrow tributaries. It was here in Pin Mill, Suffolk, that many of the barges were maintained and repaired, and because of that, the hamlet became a centre for small maritime industries such as sail making. Its nautical heart is very much still in evidence, and the boatyard remains operational today, maintaining beautiful, traditional wooden boats and helping a small sailing community thrive.

The Butt & Oyster pub has also put this sleepy backwater on the map. Dating back to the 17th century, it's one of the oldest pubs in Suffolk, the name supposedly deriving from storage of oysters in 'butts', large barrel casks. It's long been a popular spot for sailors and fishermen, and naturally, there's a strong seafood and maritime focus. As it's right on the riverfront, there's also a smuggling tale or two, and the building has been listed since the 1980s. Evidence suggests that some parts of the building were used as a court by water bailiffs as far back as the late 1400s.

THE WALK

This route is a forgiving, family-friendly one that offers up a mixture of parkland, countryside and waterside walking. It's likely that at the water's edge you'll meet a gentle scene of sailors working on their tenders amid the ebb and flow of the tide, bringing with it an abundance of birds and wildlife.

From the car park in Pin Mill, turn left and walk towards the water's edge. The pub is on your right, but you'll turn left here and go past Harry King's boatyard. This famous boatyard has an esteemed history and has built and maintained many of the beautiful barges and wooden-hulled vessels you see in this part of England. Established in the mid-1800s, it still offers comprehensive maintenance and storage services for a variety of traditional boats.

Next, you'll reach the Pin Mill Sailing Club. Turn left here, and then right at the footpath sign. Follow the path through the boat storage area and continue straight ahead, eventually emerging into fields. The river is visible through the trees on your right, and as you follow this path, you'll pass a small area of woodland before reaching Woolverstone Marina.

At the marina, there sits a small cabin that you pass, and after this, follow the sign and turn left onto the road. Pass a car park on the left and turn left as a signpost marks the Orwell Walk. Eventually, you'll emerge at the Church of St Michael. Keep to the left and follow the fence around the churchyard. Cross over a stile signed

◂ The Butt & Oyster has strong maritime connections, and is situated right on the estuary.

THE PUB: The Butt & Oyster, Pin Mill, Ipswich, Suff IP9 1JW
🌐 www.debeninns.co.uk/buttandoyster
☎ 01473 780764

START AND END POINT: Pin Mill Car Park, Chelmondiston, Ipswich, Suff IP9 1JN

WALK LENGTH: 4.8km (3 miles)

ASCENT: 44m (144ft)

APPROX. TIME: 1 hour

PARKING: Pin Mill Car Park (see above)

CAR FREE: Forresters Arms Bus Stop in Chelmondiston, Ipswich, Suff IP9 1EB

Chelmondiston, then cross diagonally to a further pair of stiles. Go over the main drive to Woolverstone Hall and follow the path alongside an iron fence.

The river will come into view again here. Continue along this path beside fields to your left – the grounds of Woolverstone Park and the impressive territory of Ipswich High School. At Park Cottages, you'll meet a small track. Cross over this and continue ahead, and before the path dips, take a signposted left back towards Pin Mill. Keep to the right, and then at the end of the path, turn right again at the T-junction and back to the boatyard and The Butt & Oyster.

▲ Pin Mill and the estuary in an evening light is an atmospheric place to be.

► The estuary here is an atmopheric place, with wooden-hulled barges lining the shores.

SOUTH-EAST

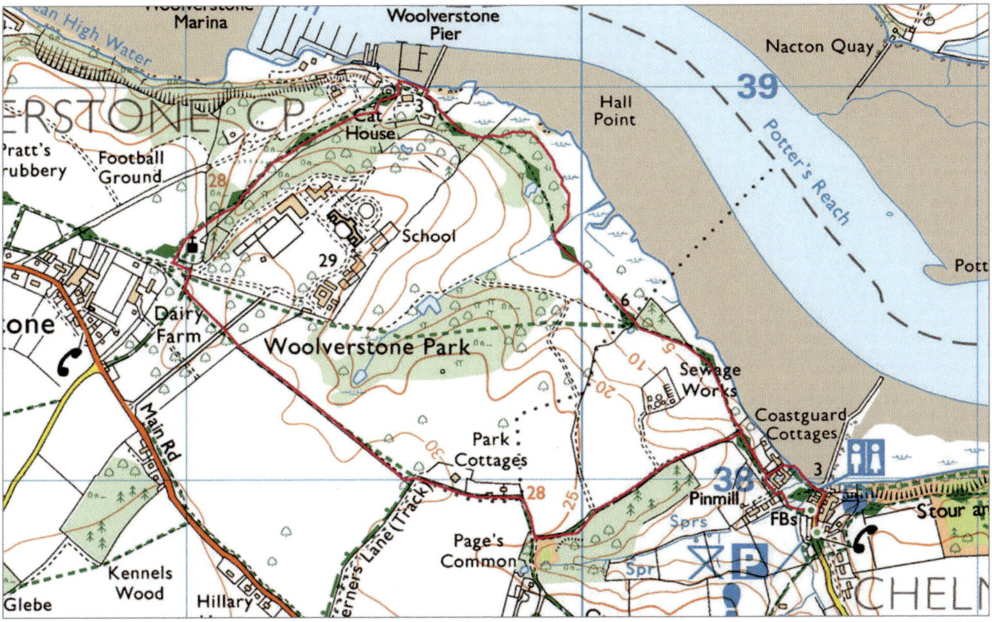
Marina
Woolverstone
Pier
Nacton Quay
39
Hall
Point
Potter's Reach
Cat
House
Football
Ground
School
29
Dairy
Farm
Woolverstone Park
Sewage
Works
Coastguard
Cottages
Park
Cottages
28
Pinmill
FBs
Main Rd
Page's
Common
Kennels
Wood
Glebe
Hillary

43

DEVIL'S DYKE & THE THREE BLACKBIRDS

— 5.8km (3.6 miles) —

Stretching through the Cambridgeshire countryside, the historic Devil's Dyke, or Devil's Ditch, is not like most footpaths. Dating to the early medieval period, it's believed to have been constructed by the Anglo-Saxons as a defensive barrier from Reach to the picturesque village of Woodditton. It's one of several Cambridgeshire Dykes, which were often used to control movement along ancient roads, determining which people and trade could cross into various territories. The path itself sits on top of a high bank, which reaches 9–10m (30–33ft) at some points – today, roads and a railway line intersect it, but cutting through open fields and some of the region's best countryside, it's not hard to imagine that much of it looks the same as it did then, linking the area and its people intimately to its earliest history.

▼ Just a few miles east of Cambridge lie large expanses of England's prosperous farmland.

The route spans nearly 12km (7.5 miles), cutting through rolling fields and dense woodland, and bridges the border between Suffolk and Cambridgeshire – the pub is in Suffolk, while the village of Woodditton sits in Cambridgeshire. It's one reason this route would have been so historically important. Local folklore suggests that these earthworks were the work of the devil himself. According to legend, the devil intended to flood the Fenlands by creating a massive trench, but his efforts were thwarted by the prayers of local villagers. Today, the trench forms part of a popular local walking route, and as many places like this in England, it's a piece of ancient history buried in an otherwise unassuming part of the countryside.

THE WALK

It's easy to get to the start of the Dyke from The Three Blackbirds at Woodditton. Turn right out the front door of the pub, and follow the road past a large water tower on your right, an imposing structure built in the 1930s to support a growing agricultural population, and still in use today. Once past the tower and round the bend, look out for a small path on your right

▲ Newmarket Racecourse dominates this flat landscape.

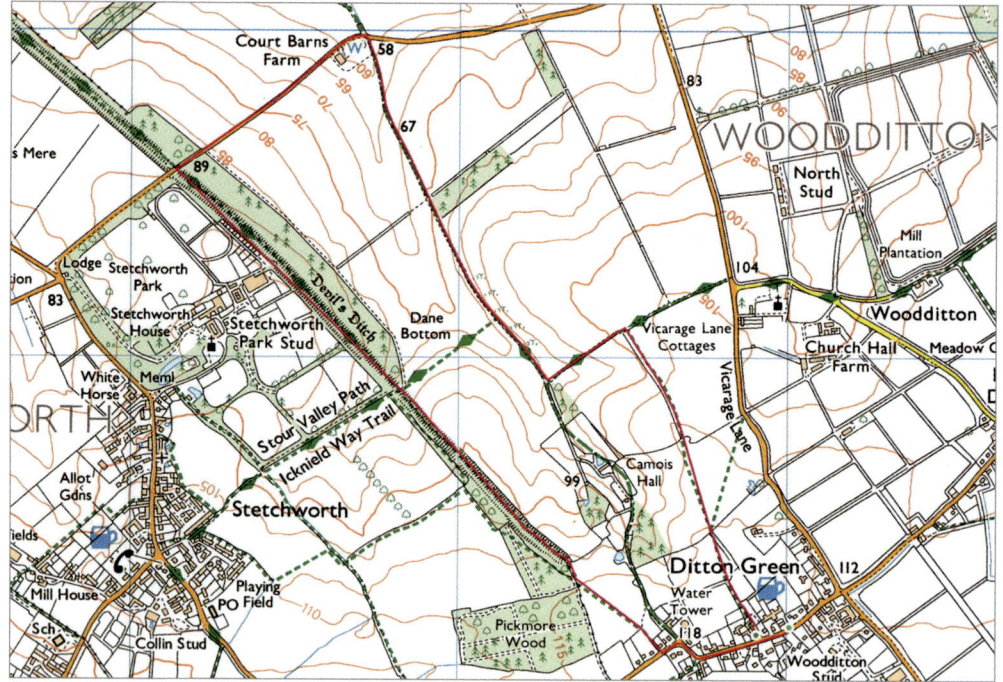

between two inconspicuous houses – there's a fingerpost here that directs you onto the Dyke.

Once on the Dyke, you can either choose to walk in a more or less straight line towards Reach for about 11km (7 miles) and back again, or for a shorter walk, doable in an afternoon, this stroll takes you past Stetchworth House on the left initially, before you need to turn right at the first small lane you come to. Instead of crossing the road, turn to the right and walk along the grass verge until you reach a large farm barn.

Just past the barn, a farm drive and a gate lead into a large field, accompanied by a series of footpath waymakers. Take this drive and walk through the gate into the open field, following the track through the rolling Cambridgeshire countryside. The sky is big here and the sheer scale of the fields provide some indication as to the industrial nature of agriculture in this part of the country. Cambridgeshire and this area of the south-east is one of the UK's most important regions for arable farming and, due to the landscape, farms are larger than average here (over 120ha/295 acres, as opposed to the national average of 88ha/217 acres). The county is a leading producer of cereals (wheat and barley) and oilseeds, and has a thriving horticultural sector, particularly in vegetable and salad crop production. Potatoes, carrots, onions and sugar beet are among the key crops.

When you reach a left-hand turn in the field, take it and follow a similarly sized dirt track, before taking the next available right down the edge of the neighbouring field. You can then cross three different fields on a well-trodden route before eventually ending up on a path that brings you back to the village of Woodditton behind the water tower.

Dating to the 17th century, The Three Blackbirds retains much of its original charm, which is a joy in itself, given the fact that the pub was devastated by a fire in 2018. Since then it has been brought back to life, with a modern and elegant twist – they have newly-built rooms you can stay in and a menu consisting of produce from artisan suppliers up and down the county.

THE PUB: The Three Blackbirds, 36 Ditton Green, Woodditton, Newmarket, Suff CB8 9SQ
🌐 www.threeblackbirds.co.uk
📞 01638 731100

START AND END POINT: The Three Blackbirds (see above)

WALK LENGTH: 5.8km (3.6 miles)

ASCENT: 64m (210ft)

APPROX. TIME: 1 hour 30 minutes

PARKING: Available at The Three Blackbirds (see above)

CAR FREE: West End Bus Stop outside the pub, from nearby villages and towns

---

▼ The Three Blackbirds still holds plenty of classic charm alongside it's modern rebuilding.

44

HAMBLEDEN, PHEASANT'S HILL & THE STAG & HUNTSMAN

— 4.8km (3 miles) —

The great migration out of London, to the nearby countryside, is one of southern England's most defining features of the 20th century. Berkshire, Buckinghamshire and Oxfordshire are three of the regions that make up what we now know as the home counties, named as such for being the most desirable locations for an elite class of London workers to call home. As transportation routes have improved, so desirability has spread further from the capital.

▼ Hambleden is tucked away in a valley next to the prosperous town of Henley-on-Thames.

Within this area lies the Chiltern Hills, and in some places it's possible to spot a hint of how England may have looked before such a high concentration of wealth was gathered here. Hambleden is a small village within the hills that nudges up against Henley-on-Thames; and it's a place that's been preserved and maintained and, against the grain, has changed very little across much of the last century. It's so renowned for its timeless qualities that it has often been used as a film location due to its unspoiled and classic countryside appearance – it's easy to spot in the 1968 film *Chitty Chitty Bang Bang* and long-running TV series *Midsomer Murders*, to name just two.

Hambleden's history is deeply rooted in its agricultural past. The village is named in the Domesday Book of 1086 as 'Hanbledene', so it's clear there's been a settlement here for a long time. The name Hambleden is believed to be derived from the Old English words *hamel*, meaning 'crooked' or 'flat-topped', and *denu*, meaning 'valley'. Over the centuries, the village developed around its agricultural economy and farming played a central role in community life.

Well-preserved architecture is at Hambleden's heart and the village is home to several historic buildings, including St Mary the Virgin Church, while there's also an array of traditional cottages, many of which are constructed from flint and brick, characteristic of the Chilterns area. Lots of the houses are estate

workers' cottages, and would have been busy with farmhands in days gone by, with The Stag & Huntsman pub serving as their social hub. Any hint of spit and sawdust has long since departed the pub though, and having been recently refurbished by a small hotel chain, there are well-appointed cottages and rooms to welcome you should you wish to stay the night. Thankfully, it's still a proper English boozer at heart; there's a cosy bar area and a decent garden out the back.

THE WALK

This short circular walk is a perfect family stroll with the dogs – not too taxing, but enough to stretch your legs before a pint and lunch. Park in the car park behind the pub and turn right up the little lane, ascending into the woodland. Continue going up, and you'll soon emerge into a clearing with farm buildings on your right. Keep going straight, past the imposing, grand driveway at Hutton Farm and its small adjoining paddocks, before you reach a small country lane.

At the lane, which leads from Mill End up to the village of Freith, turn left and continue a short way, past a farmhouse on your left. Once you reach the entrance into Heath Wood, turn left and continue along this sometimes-muddy woodland track until you reach a junction at North Close Copse plantation. With good views across the valley, you're likely to spot collections of deer in neighbouring fields, and as the name suggests, lots of pheasants. You're now heading towards Pheasant's Hill;

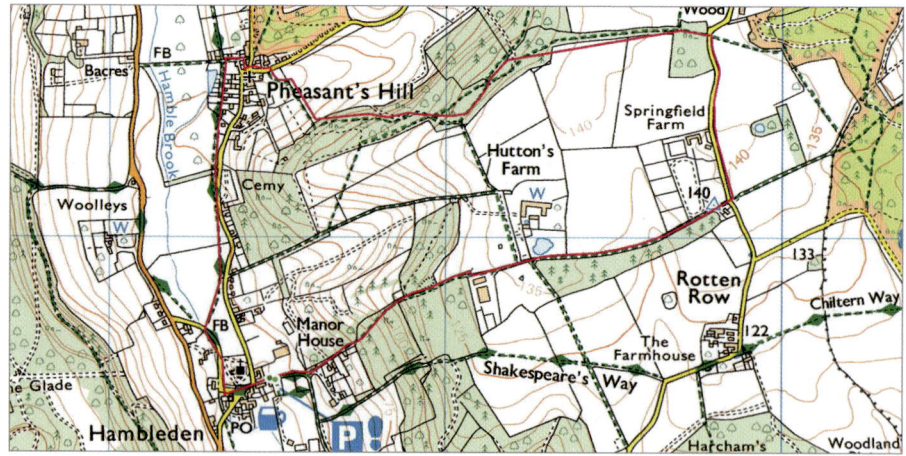

► The Stag & Huntsman has sat at the heart of the Hambleden community for generations.

THE PUB: The Stag & Huntsman, Hambleden, Henley-on-Thames, Oxon RG9 6RP
www.stagandhuntsman.com
01491 571227

START AND END POINT: The Stag & Huntsman (see above)

WALK LENGTH: 4.8km (3 miles)

ASCENT: 107m (351ft)

APPROX. TIME: 1 hour 15 minutes

PARKING: Available at The Stag & Huntsman (see above)

CAR FREE: Mill End Bus Stop for routes from Henley and surrounding areas

▲ To this day, the large church in the village is at the centre of the community.

keep going on the path you were on out of the plantation and when you reach a crossroads, take a right downhill, ending up next to two fields with stables in front of you and a sharp right-hand turn.

Take the path along the edge of the horse fields and then up opposite two quaint cottages with steps leading up to the front doors. Turn left down the hill and then almost immediately right, skirting the main hamlet of Pheasant's Hill. Here, you turn left among a collection of houses, and then left again to join the path at the bottom of the gardens of the houses you've just walked past, next to Hamble Brook. From here, it's a clear route back to the church at Hambleden, and then a left back up to the pub.

I confess to a personal connection to this pub as it has family ties – my mum worked here in the late 1970s, so I note its appearance with interest – what's changed? What's stayed the same? Thankfully, there's a homely feel and I can instantly imagine the rural atmosphere here all those years ago. Needless to say, there's the sense that Hambleden, despite the ever-increasing wealth that surrounds it, stubbornly refuses to alter. As I said, a little bit of old south-east England hidden within a pocket of otherwise enormous prosperity.

▲ The welcoming bar area of the pub has retained much of its traditional charm.

45

SHERE & THE WHITE HORSE

— 5.8km (3.6 miles) —

With its patchwork of white and brick buildings, timber-framed cottages, little lanes and a bustling local community, Shere represents a certain style of quintessential English charm. Just 48km (30 miles) south-west of London, the village itself has a somewhat celebrated life as a Hollywood film location. It has served as a backdrop for several films and television shows, most notably *The Holiday*, *Bridget Jones* and *Four Weddings and a Funeral*. Essentially, if you want something to look 'English', you come here.

▼ The *Flying Scotsman* passes the village of Shere on its way through the Surrey countryside.

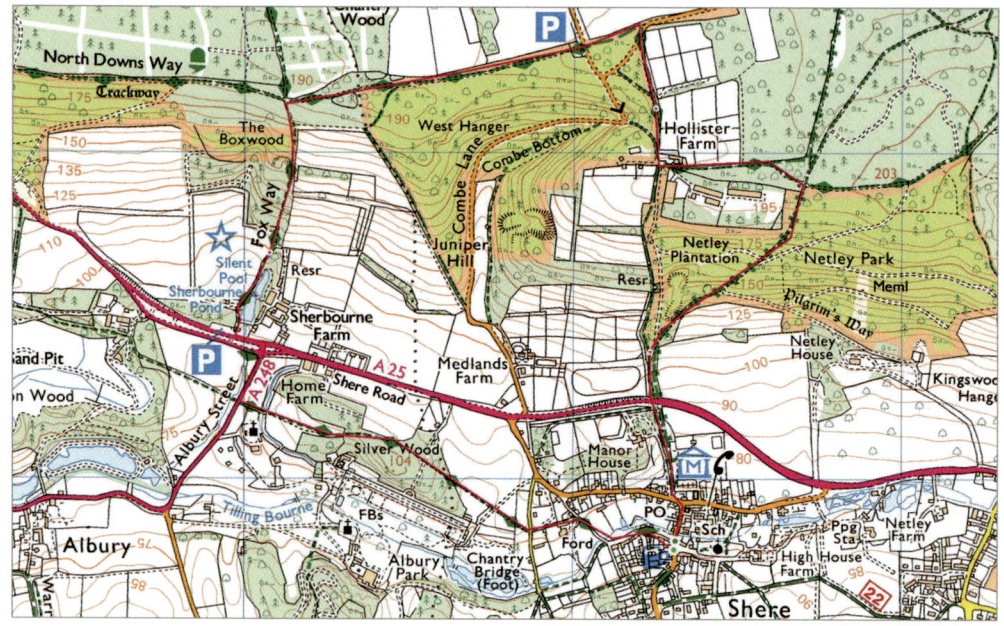

The history of Shere dates to the Domesday Book of 1086, where it was recorded as 'Essira'. The village is dominated by the 12th-century St James Church, a beautiful example of Norman architecture, which is flanked by narrow, winding streets, many houses and buildings showcasing old thatched roofs and cottage gardens blooming out front. The Shere Museum offers an insight into local history, showcasing artifacts and exhibits that span from prehistoric times to present day.

The village itself often ranks near the top in lists of England's most beautiful villages, while it also boasts access to the Surrey Hills, a protected landscape of common land, woodland and forest that belies its location so close to England's capital.

THE WALK

This walk takes in some of the Surrey Hills area, initially following the banks of the pretty River Tillingbourne, which flows through Shere. From the village's centre, with The White Horse pub in front of you, take Lower Street past the pub, following a lane with willows next to the river on your right and black timber buildings on your left. Continue along Lower Street, with pretty houses on your left and an array of vegetable patches beyond an old stone wall on your right. Keep to the right and ford the river. Going straight across the lane, you soon reach Silver Wood. Don't deviate from this track until you reach a busy road – the A248 (there's a path next to the road so you don't have to fight with the traffic). Cross the busy junction with the A25, then venture left and immediately right into the car park for Silent Pool.

There's an enchanting feeling at Silent Pool, at odds with the relatively cosmopolitan backdrop. It's said that a woodcutter's daughter drowned here while attempting to avoid the advances of King John, but whatever the story, it's a beautiful spot of water that often gets busy during tourist season. Past the pool, continue along the Fox Way sharply uphill towards the North Downs Way.

This part of the North Downs Way was built by Canadian soldiers during the First World War. Enjoy the views from the top before heading into the woodland and turning right through dense trees, eventually reaching a car park. Go past the car park and turn right, down towards Hollister Farm, skirting its edge into Netley plantation and a portion of the Pilgrim's Way. To give away this walk's location, look out for the pillboxes that housed anti-aircraft guns to defend London from aerial invasion during the Second World War. Follow this route south, and downhill, before crossing the A25 again, back down to the centre of the village.

Finishing the walk at The White Horse, you'll find yourself in one of the oldest pubs in Surrey, dating to the 15th century. According to local lore, the pub is haunted by a friendly ghost – legend has it that the spirit of a former landlord, who was particularly fond of the premises, still lingers here. You may also recognise

▲ Silent Pool is fed by underground springs, and has an eerie stillness that draws visitors throughout the year.

THE PUB: The White Horse, Shere Lane, Shere, Guildford, Sy GU5 9HS
www.chefandbrewer.com/pubs/surrey/white-horse
01483 202518

START AND END POINT: Shere Car Park, Shere, Guildford, Sy GU5 9HE

WALK LENGTH: 5.8km (3.6 miles)

ASCENT: 148m (486ft)

APPROX. TIME: 1 hour 30 minutes

PARKING: Shere Car Park (see above)

CAR FREE: Shere Village Hall bus stops located on Gomshall Lane GU5 9HE

the pub from the 2006 rom-com *The Holiday*, but perhaps more fascinating, it's also believed to contain timbers from Nelson's flagship, *Victory*. Like all taverns of its ilk, its nooks and crannies house old tales of smuggling and petty theft, but today it's a charming way to end a walk in some of England's most delightful countryside. On a sunny day, there's also a lovely courtyard to soak up the best of British pub life.

▼ Shere is a picture-book version of a rural English town, despite its proximity to London. The charming timbered facade of The White Horse is visible in the distance.

46

BEACON HILL & THE THREE HORSESHOES

— 6.6km (4.1 miles) —

As one of the highest points on the South Downs, Beacon Hill is well worth the climb. As the starting point for this walk, the village of Elsted sits on top of a ridge at the western end of the Sussex High Weald and the place hosts a thriving rural community. The charmingly excellent Three Horseshoes pub provides an important focal point for village life, and it's also the start and end point of this walk.

The village of Elsted itself dates back several centuries, with its most notable landmark, St Paul's Church, built in the 19th century and replacing an earlier medieval structure. The village plays host to the start of the popular walk up Beacon Hill, and rising to an elevation of 242m (794ft), it offers some of the most breathtaking views in the region – but make no mistake, it can be steep in places. As a hillfort, it dates back to the late Bronze Age and is named after the ancient beacons that were once lit on its summit to warn of impending invasions. On a clear day, the vistas extend as far as the Isle of Wight to the south and the rolling hills of the South Downs to the east and west.

▼ This area of Harting Down and Beacon Hill has countless walking routes with great views across the Sussex countryside.

THE WALK

Start by parking at The Three Horseshoes and heading down the little slope and southwards, before you reach the village centre, where old ivy-clad buildings and parish noticeboards watch over a sleepy scene. Turn left, descending on a small lane that gets increasingly wooded with peaceful cottages and farm buildings fringing its borders. Before long the views start to open out as you get into countryside proper, and as the road bears sharply round to the left, continue straight on to the unpaved farm track that acts as a footpath to begin the climb to the Beacon.

As you enter a woodland, you'll be greeted by a choice of paths – turn right and continue straight ahead along the (steep!) path that works its way directly to the summit of the Beacon. The views once you reach the Downs are impressive, and from the top, after a short break, continue on towards the National Trust-managed Harting Down, with wildflowers and grasslands bordering the chalky path.

When you reach a choice of pathways, follow the ridge line down to Little Round Down, turning left at a crossroads to bring your journey northwards. At the junction, turn right towards Telegraph House, and once you reach a small patch of woodland, turn left at the house to round the other side of the Beacon and head back to the path you came in on. Once you reach the plantation again, it's a simple exercise to follow the path and road back to the pub.

Once back at the pub, you're greeted by a quaint, vine-cloaked building that seems to have leapt straight from the pages of a storybook. Its traditional brick and timber is well maintained,

THE PUB: The Three Horseshoes, Elsted, Midhurst, W. Ssx GU29 0JY
🌐 www.3hs.co.uk
📞 01730 825746

START AND END POINT: The Three Horseshoes (see above)

WALK LENGTH: 6.6km (4.1 miles)

ASCENT: 269m (883ft)

APPROX. TIME: 2 hours

PARKING: Available at The Three Horseshoes (see above)

CAR FREE: Buses from Petersfield and surrounding areas – bus stops on Elsted Rd

and inside, the low-beamed ceilings, rustic wooden furniture and crackling open fireplace create an intimate and inviting ambience. It's cosy in the winter, but even better in the summer, thanks to one of the standout features being the breathtaking views from its garden. Nestled at the foot of the South Downs, the pub boasts panoramic vistas that stretch across rolling hills and countryside. The menu celebrates the best of British cuisine, with a focus on locally-sourced, seasonal ingredients from copious producers in the area. An old-fashioned traditional country pub, with a wonderful garden that caters for the whole family – it's a gem.

▼ The Three Horseshoes offers a cosy space to sit and look out to the rolling countryside.

47

FIRLE BEACON & THE RAM INN

— 8.2km (5.1 miles) —

The name 'Firle' refers to an old Anglo-Saxon word, *fierol*, meaning 'overgrown with oak', and it feels like the name suits this tree-lined village, which sits at the foot of the South Downs and at the start of the route up to the highest peak in the area, Firle Beacon.

Park at The Ram Inn, a 16th-century pub that sits right at the heart of the village. It's a proper country pub and B&B, not unlike many in this region of the south-east. 'At the bar you'll find artists, walkers, writers, farmers, farriers and vicars,' say the owners on their website, and it's true that the establishment is a home from home for a wide array of people working in this village.

▼ The rolling hills of the South Downs from Firle Beacon.

THE WALK

From the pub, walk away from it towards the cottage-lined road, heading for its centre and the post office and stores. Here, ahead of you, you'll see a small overgrown path that leads to the church. It's worth a diversion down here; the graveyard is purposely unkempt and left to wild. During spring and summer, nature takes over and intertwines with the gravestones, which provides a lovely start to the walk. Look out for many generations of the Gage family, who still live in and look after the Firle country estate and park.

Back out of the church, follow the road around until it reaches more of a track than a paved surface. There are farm buildings on your left and right that house Burning Sky Brewery. Although its beers can be sampled across the trendier parts of the cities of England, it's a proper farmhouse operation here, and worth remembering for when you get back to the pub.

The path quickly turns into the old coach road; follow this around to the left, then take a right towards Firle plantation. Ignoring the entrance to the plantation itself, bear around to the left and follow the path closest to the fence line, emerging onto open land that then climbs steeply uphill to the Beacon. You're now over 200m (656ft) up after the climb – turn left on top of the ridge to reach the trig point. Great views across to the Channel and the South Downs can be enjoyed from up here, and you may well share the spot with a paraglider or two if conditions are right. On a calm, sunny evening, it's a favourite spot for them, and the silent, gliding dots peppered across the sky above you is quite a sight.

Continue walking from the trig point

▶ The South Downs offers stunning views and walks aplenty!

SOUTH-EAST

218

until the path starts veering around to the right and slightly downhill. Keep going straight until you reach a small car park at Bopeep Farm, or, for a more direct route, take the left-hand turn, which is a steep downhill path but the most direct route down. They both lead to pretty much the same place.

Assuming you carried on to the car park, the less steep version of the walk sees you turn down the road that leads to it – walk until you reach large buildings at Bopeep Farm. At a junction, there is a long, flat path on your left that leads across neighbouring farmland, signposted

THE PUB: The Ram Inn, Firle, Lewes,
E. Ssx BN8 6NS
🌐 www.raminn.co.uk
📞 01273 858222

START AND END POINT: The Ram Inn (see above)

WALK LENGTH: 8.2km (5.1 miles)

ASCENT: 237m (778ft)

APPROX. TIME: 2 hours

PARKING: Firle Village Car Park, Firle, Lewes, E. Ssx BN8 6NS

CAR FREE: Firle Park Gates Bus Stop, Lewes, E. Ssx BN8 6LG

'Firle'. Take this path, looking up at the Beacon and the paragliders circling above you. Stay on this route past Round Hill, picking up the rough coach track that you left earlier. Enter back into Firle from where you left, and retrace your steps to the pub.

Once back in the village, it'll feel like you've returned to a quiet backwater; there's very little here aside from the pretty cottages, the church, post office and, of course, the pub. The lack of streetlights, any road markings or any through traffic speak to an England of a different era. If someone told me I had been transported back to 1942, I would have believed them. The rambling old brick and flint pub building has three rooms for wining and dining, each with its own open fire. It gets busy here at weekends, as it's well-known for the quality of its menu, but it's also the place for a decent pint in quiet surroundings; decadent and smart without being pretentious, with a handsome selection of local produce, beers, wines and spirits.

▼ The Ram Inn has three main rooms, each with an open fire that is lit everyday between October and April.

SOUTH-EAST

48

BIRLING GAP, BEACHY HEAD & THE TIGER INN

— 12km (7.5 miles) —

There is something about walking towards Birling Gap and Beachy Head that makes you feel like you're walking towards the edge of the world. It's the point at which England just stops – not as it does in places like Cornwall and Devon, where craggy, gnarled cliffs weave around the coastline, but sharply, dramatically and abruptly. These huge white chalk cliffs, known as the Seven Sisters, act as luminous sentinels on the southern coast of England – and are often visible from France. Their defiant symbolism is perhaps just as famous as the cliffs themselves, and in person, they're almost as theatrical as legend would suggest, forming the southern façade of the South Downs National Park and sitting below the newly opened King Charles III England Coast Path. Natural England has been working in partnership with local authorities around the country to create the path, which will allow – for the first time – walking access to all 4,345km (2,700 miles) of England's coastline. This section is now open, and others are on their way. When complete, it will be the longest managed coast path in the world.

► Beachy Head Lighthouse is one of the most recognisable spots in southern England.

THE WALK

In the village of East Dean, you'll find a quaint village green, fringed on all sides by large cottages often seen in this part of England, as well as The Tiger Inn, a quintessential, low-slung, oak-beamed pub. Park near the pub, and opposite the village green turn right on the road, following it round to the right (this may have been the road you came in on) and then left uphill on a path next to a waymarked sign.

Follow the footpath straight up towards Hobb's Eares, and at the top, after a short steep section, look back and you'll see great views of East Dean and on towards the coastline, including Belle Tout Lighthouse, the precursor to the larger lighthouse at Beachy Head. You'll soon reach Crowlink Road and the National Trust car park – go through the gate and follow the path with the fence line on your left.

Through the next fence line, the path veers to the right and crosses over the top of Went Hill, now heading towards the sea. Birling Gap hamlet will be in front of you as you turn left towards the visitor area.

The Seven Sisters, stark white against the sea, are best enjoyed from slightly further up the coast path as you look back on this dramatic landscape. But to appreciate their size, it's also worth climbing down the staircase and visiting the centre here to learn more about their composition. The swales in the cliffs – the dips you see in between each cliff – are the remnants of dry

▼ The chalk cliffs here draw visitors from all over the globe, and are an impressive icon of the British isles.

valleys in the South Downs that the sea has been eroding over thousands of years. The ecosystem is delicate here, and the inevitable erosion of these soft chalk cliffs still takes place at an alarming rate.

Continue towards the lighthouse on the clear coastal path, and then beyond this, spot Beachy Head Lighthouse at the foot of the cliffs. The lighthouse was built at the bottom of the cliffs to improve visibility and help ships navigate the coastline here. It was the last offshore rock tower lighthouse of its type to be built by Trinity House, and is arguably one of the most famous lighthouses in the world, and thanks to a campaign to raise money to keep repainting it, it still boasts its trademark red and white stripes.

Beyond Beachy Head at the car park and visitor centre, the route now veers inland and follows the road. At a T-Junction on the path, turn right and head inland, traversing the undulating hills of the South Downs, the furrows as you head into the countryside are in stark contrast to the drama of the cliff edges. On the way back, keep ahead, not

> **THE PUB:** The Tiger Inn, The Green, East Dean, Eastbourne, E. Ssx BN20 0DA
> 🌐 www.beachyhead.org.uk/the-tiger-inn
> 📞 01323 423209
>
> **START AND END POINT:** East Dean Village Green, East Dean, Eastbourne, E. Ssx BN20 0BY
>
> **WALK LENGTH:** 12km (7.5 miles)
>
> **ASCENT:** 360m (1,181ft)
>
> **APPROX. TIME:** 3 hours
>
> **PARKING:** East Dean Village Green (see above)
>
> **CAR FREE:** The Eastbourne to Brighton Coaster (bus service) stops at East Dean

▼ The Tiger Inn, at the heart of the village of East Dean.

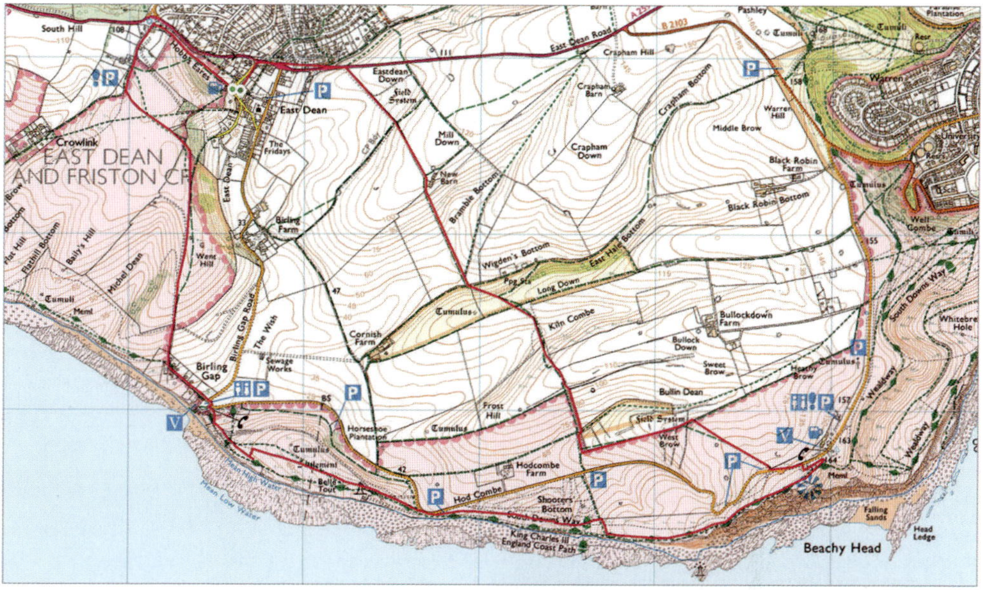

deviating from the path you're on and walking across combes in the valleys, and past the occasional track and farm building. At the end of the path you'll reach the main road just east of East Dean, and you can turn left and follow this back to the pub.

The Tiger Inn boasts its village green, which provides a handsome place to sit with a pint on a sunny day. There's also a small café here, a deli and a collection of old-fashioned cottages to wander around; not least the supposed retirement home of Sherlock Holmes, as written into Arthur Conan Doyle's books, resplendent with a blue plaque of its own. The menu at the pub is elevated British flair, and there are several snugs and dining room areas in which to enjoy a hearty meal and a pint or two. It's best on a sunny day though, when you can enjoy the breeze that sweeps off south-east England's most impressive cliffs.

▲ The pub is tastefully decorated, and hosts a thriving lunch scene for hungry walkers.

49

RYE & THE PLAYDEN OASTS INN

— 4.7km (2.9 miles) —

It would feel remiss to include a collection of walks in south-east England without embracing a walk to arguably one of the region's most recognisable buildings, the oast house. Designed for drying hops as part of the brewing process, oast houses are seen peppered across the countryside of beer-making counties – in other parts of England, you're likely to hear them being described as hop kilns.

The earliest surviving oast house is not far away from this walk, near Tunbridge Wells, and it dates from the 17th century, which is not long after the introduction of hops into this country. The Playden Oasts Inn, located near Rye, is unusual partly because it's a pub in an oast house, but also because it's open to the public. In the past, many oast houses were bought up as pieces of quirky real estate, and often turned into houses and hotels. Believed to be built in 1800 to aid in the creation of local real ale, The Playden Oasts has been renovated, and you can stay in the building as well as choose to eat in one of two restaurant areas, one of which is pet-friendly. It's got a generous beer garden, too.

THE WALK

The pub walk starts not at the pub but outside, nearby Rye railway station, meaning you get to enjoy the cobbled streets of England's 'medieval citadel' as part of the short stroll around the Tillingham Valley. At the station, turn right to follow the road running parallel with the railway line, and at the road junction, turn right along Ferry Road. Passing underneath the railway, you shortly find a right-hand turn onto a signed footpath. Continue on

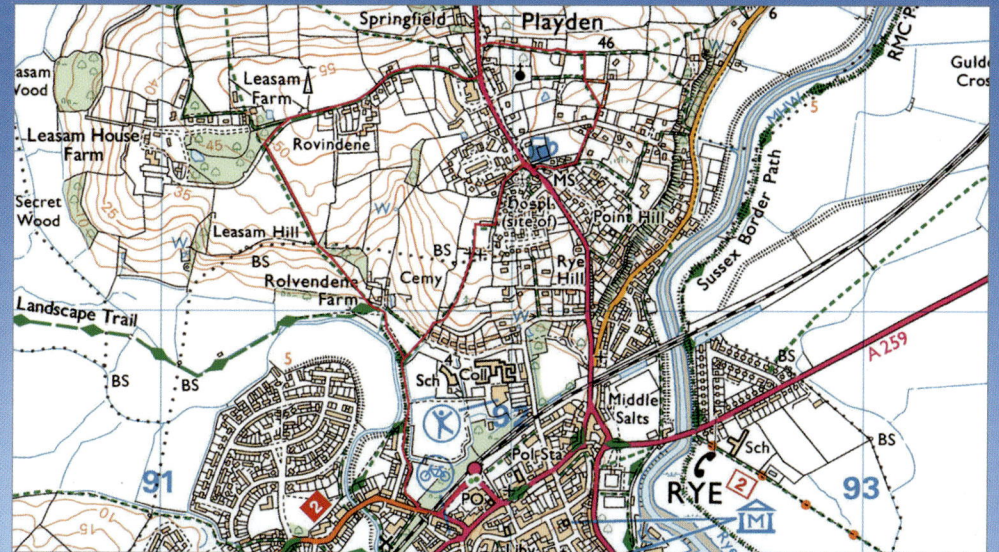

to Tillingham Avenue, then when the road runs out, take the surfaced footpath along the banks of the river.

Keep bearing right and when you reach a road called Love Lane, go through a kissing gate on the left and keep going past Rolvendene Farm.

Ignore the footpath to the left and head uphill beside the farmhouse – you'll reach a gate. Go through the gate, keeping the field boundary on your right, and then after a stile, continue along the edge of the next field to reach Leasam Lane.

▼ The Playden Oasts Inn was built in 1800 and originally used as a working oast house to dry locally grown hops.

▲ The cobbled streets of Rye transport you to an ancient version of England.

Turn right here and follow the lane to its junction with the main A268 road. This is the final stretch to the pub; turn left and follow the road but be sure to cross the road and stay on the footpath, which is situated a distance back from the road, as there's a constant supply of traffic. Before long, you'll reach a driveway – turn right and you'll be in The Playden Oasts car park.

Once you're finished at the pub, go back the way you came on the main road footpath until you reach a turning on your left signposted Rectory Lane. After a few hundred yards, turn right onto the signposted footpath and cross the field to a gate that leads onto a driveway. A few steps after turning left, the driveway bears around again to the left and the path goes right, through a gate and on across New England Lane. Keep going until you reach Salcote Lane. Turn right, and cross over the A268 again.

Once you've crossed the road, continue along the signposted route to the cemetery. Past the cottage, turn right at the footpath and go alongside a hedge, turning left and towards the large yew tree between the two chapel buildings. You can then follow a gravel driveway to the edge of the cemetery and a kissing gate. After a short distance across a small field, the path descends

► The rooftops of Rye.

a flight of steps to return to the edge of the driveway leading to Rolvendene Farm. Back through the kissing gate and across Love Lane, you can then retrace your steps back to Rye to explore its impressive array of preserved architecture and ancient backstreets.

Rye's history is deeply intertwined with its strategic location near the English Channel. In the 13th century, it became one of the Cinque Ports, a confederation of maritime towns vital for defence and trade. This status brought prosperity and the town's importance continued through the centuries, despite challenges from French raids.

It feels like stepping back in time here. The town is compact and easily walkable, with the historic core dominated by cobbled streets and half-timbered houses. Mermaid Street, perhaps the most famous street in Rye, is lined with charming medieval and Tudor buildings, and during the year, if you do this walk at the right time, you'll be greeted by hundreds of different activities and community events – many of them with a historic twist. The Rye Arts Festival and Rye Bonfire Night draw large crowds and are especially impressive occasions.

THE PUB: The Playden Oasts Inn, Rye Road, Playden, Rye, E. Ssx TN31 7UL
🌐 www.playdenoast.co.uk
📞 01797 223502

START AND END POINT: Rye train station, Station Approach, Rye, E. Ssx TN31 7AB

WALK LENGTH: 4.7km (2.9 miles)

ASCENT: 76m (249ft)

APPROX. TIME: 1 hour 10 minutes

PARKING: Rye train station (see above)

CAR FREE: There are several bus stops at the train station, on Station Approach, Rye TN31 7AB

50

DOWN WOOD FROM CHILHAM & THE WHITE HORSE INN

— 7.2km (4.5 miles) —

In deepest south-east England, near the ancient and historic city of Canterbury, sits Chilham. The village itself has deeply historic roots, offering up a perfect slice of British history as well as great links to the surrounding Kent Downs for day walks.

Chilham's history – and that of the area as a whole – is inextricably linked to its strategic location and its most notable landmark, Chilham Castle. The village sits on the ancient road between Canterbury and Ashford, significant since Roman times due to its location on the pilgrimage route to Canterbury Cathedral, drawing travellers, commerce and a large amount of trade to the area. The castle site has been fortified since at least Norman times and the

current castle is largely a Jacobean mansion built around a Norman keep, with its construction dating back to the early 17th century when it was reshaped by Sir Dudley Digges, a merchant adventurer and close friend of William Shakespeare. The keep itself is a relic of the original Norman castle, and dates to the 12th century. The entire site was once owned by Henry VIII, and has been an exclusive private residence for nearly five centuries.

Not only is there a feeling of deep historical importance in Chilham, but it's also a beautiful place, with its ancient square surrounded by half-timbered houses and charming cottages that seem frozen in time. The parish church of St Mary, which dates back to the 15th century, is built on the site of an earlier Saxon church and its interior features fascinating memorials and tombs, including the tomb of Sir Dudley Digges. The market square, where you park and where The White Horse Inn sits, feels little changed from the era of medieval trade that so characterised this village.

▲ The White Horse stands among typical Kent architecture and cottage garden appeal.

◄ The woodlands around Kent offer plenty of hidden opportunities for walkers.

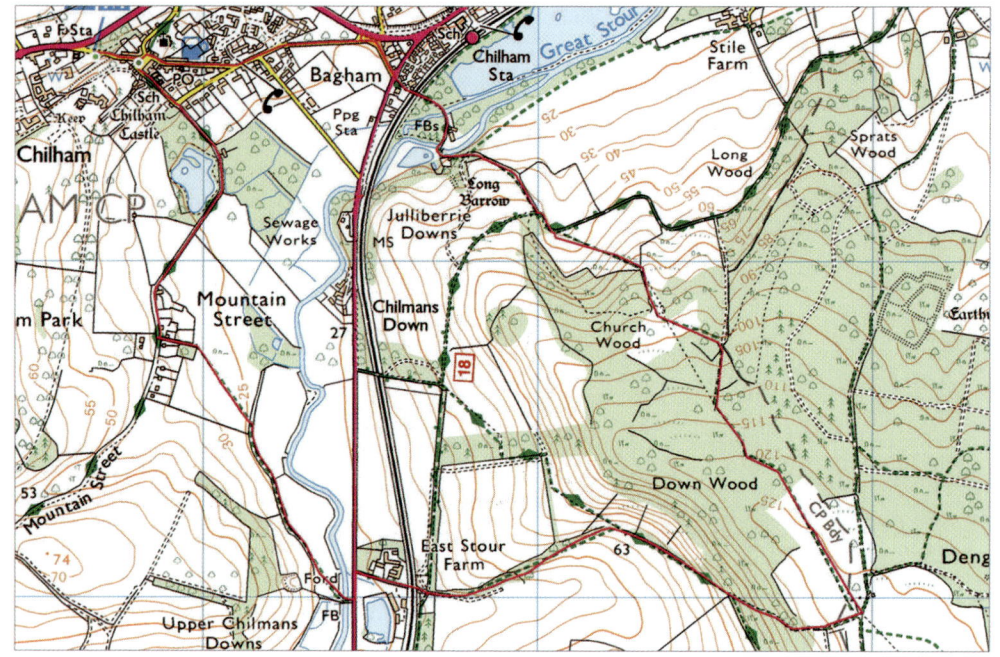

THE WALK

This walk starts at The White Horse Inn, where you'll begin by walking east, following a small, narrow lane towards the Woolpack Inn, at which point you'll join a larger road that continues on to the A252. Stay on Bagham Lane and bear round to the right, at which point you'll reach a junction with Ashford Road and a level-crossing sign in front of you. Walk straight across the road, over the railway and onto a smaller, wooded lane with historic houses to your left and right, Chilham Mill, and bodies of water from the Great Stour, the river that eventually leads through Canterbury and out to sea near Ramsgate.

When you reach a gate next to a private house, bear round to the left and keep following a narrow path that leads uphill through a woodland. This path eventually emerges to the left of a large field – keep going and continue through the gate into the next field, at which point you'll take the middle path that leads directly through the field itself – you'll see it's a well-worn route.

Aiming for the patch of trees on the other side of the field, go into the woodland and into Down Wood. At the

▶ The charming, sleepy lanes of Chilham.

right time of year this is picture-perfect bluebell territory. You'll emerge from the woods in more of a clearing – the site of a grass airstrip. Here, bear around to the right, past another small patch of woodland, before turning right at the next large field, following its edge back west, where after about 1.6km (1 mile) you'll reach the railway again and East Stour Farm.

At the farm, you'll find units that house a butchers and a farm feed business – continue on to the road and turn left onto the grass verge, watching for traffic, before almost immediately turning right through a wooden gate into some trees. Across the river, follow the left-hand side of the next field and the middle of the following one, which leads you back to a small lane with houses, known as Mountain Street. Turn right and follow the path northwards, until you return to the centre of Chilham.

> **THE PUB:** The White Horse Inn, The Square, Chilham, Canterbury, Kent CT4 8BY
> www.thewhitehorse.pub
> 01227 730355
>
> **START AND END POINT:** Chilham Car Park, Taylors Hill, Chilham, Canterbury, Kent CT4 8BZ
> **WALK LENGTH:** 7.2km (4.5 miles)
> **ASCENT:** 150m (492ft)
> **APPROX. TIME:** 1 hour 45 minutes
> **PARKING:** Chilham Car Park (see above)
> **CAR FREE:** Taylors Hill bus stop on the A252 outside Chilham

ACKNOWLEDGEMENTS

This book wouldn't have been possible without the support and constant encouragement I've received from all my friends and family. Thank you.

I'd also like to thank the pubs I contacted in the making of this book, all of which responded to the idea and concept with overwhelming positivity. Thank you in particular to those pubs who sourced images, suggested walks and welcomed me into their businesses and homes with such warmth and generosity. It has never been easy to be a landlord, and today it's even harder for small businesses to thrive, so thank you to all of you for allowing me to champion the pubs that form the heart of your communities.

Thank you to Elizabeth Multon and Kathryn Savage at Bloomsbury, who worked with me to bring this book to life and worked especially hard behind the scenes to enable what you see here to be produced.

Lastly, to my wife Sian, and daughter Sylvia, who every day encourage me to pursue what I love and give me a reason to do it. Thank you for everything you do.

PHOTO CREDITS

All photography © Jacob Little, with the exception of the following:

Adobe Stock: 4, 30, 38, 51, 52, 53, 58, 62, 78, 88, 90, 91, 92, 93, 94, 98, 118, 119, 121, 122, 124, 143, 144, 145, 190, 199, 204, 211, 214, 217, 219, 221, 227,

Flickr: 114, 116, 120, 168, 216

Geograph: 76, 101(top), 115, 123, 165, 200, 213

Getty: 87, 101(bottom), 125, 127, 130, 155, 166, 180(top right), 196, 198, 201, 209, 212, 230, 233

iStock: 156, 228, 229, 231

Wikimedia: 110

INDEX

Acorn Inn, Evershot, Dorset 147, 152, 154–5
Alwin River, Northumberland 72–6
Alwinton, Northumberland 72–5
Avebury & Silbury Hill, Wiltshire 142–5

Bamburgh Circular, Seahouses to, Northumberland 64–7
Bamburgh, Northumberland 58
Beachy Head & Birling Gap, 190, 221–5
Beacon Hill, Sussex 213–16
Birling Gap & Beachy Head, 221–5
Black Hill, Herefordshire 129–32
Black Moss Pot from Stonethwaite, Lake District 20–3
Black Mountains 129–32
Blakey Ridge & Rosedale Railway, North Yorkshire 89–91
Blue Bell Inn, Belchford, Lincolnshire 121, 122, 123, 124
Blue Bell Inn, Kettlewell, North Yorkshire 41, 44
Britannia Inn, Lake District 24, 26–7
Bugsworth Basin, Peak District 103, 108
Bull's Head, Craswall, Herefordshire 103, 129, 130, 131–2
Butt & Oyster, Pin Mill, Suffolk 196, 197, 198

Cadgwith Cove Inn, Cadgwith, Cornwall 173, 175–6, 184
Caer Caradoc, Shropshire 125–8
Cambridgeshire 200–3
Caudron, Staffordshire 112–16
Central & Northern England 102–45
Cheshire 54–7
Chilham, Kent 230–3
Chiltern Hills 205–8
Cornwall 146, 169–81, 186–9
Cotswolds 102, 134–7
Craster, Dunstanburgh Castle, Low Newton-by-the-Sea, Northumberland 68–9, 71

Cross Fell, Cumbria 14, 16, 18–19
Cumbria 15, 16–32

Dartmoor National Park, Devon 147, 160–4
Derbyshire 104–11
Devil's Dyke, Cambridgeshire 200–3
Devon 146, 147, 160–8
Dorset 147, 152–9
Down Wood from Chilham, Kent 230–3
Drake Stone at Harbottle, Northumberland 76–9
Driftwood Spars, St Agnes, Cornwall 169, 171–2

Edale Circular, Peak District 104–7
Elton and Fotheringhay, Northamptonshire 138–41

Falcon Inn, Fotheringhay, Northamptonshire 138, 140–1
Fauconberg, Thirsk Bank, North Yorkshire 97, 99, 101
Firle Beacon, Sussex 190, 217–20
Fotheringhay & Elton, Northamptonshire 138–41

Gloucestershire 134–7
Great Whernside, North Yorkshire 41–3
Greenhaugh Circular, Northumberland 80–4
Greg's Hut, Cross Fell, Cumbria 18–19

Hambleden & Pheasant's Hill, Oxfordshire 191, 204–8
Harbottle, Northumberland 76–9
Hebden Bridge, West Yorkshire 50–3
Helhoughton & Raynham, Norfolk 192–5
Herefordshire 129–33
Hole of Horcum, North Yorkshire 94–6

Holly Bush Inn, Greenhaugh, Northumberland 80–1, 82–4
Holy Island Circular, Northumberland 60–3
Horseshoe Inn, Levisham, North Yorkshire 93–4, 95, 96

Industrial Revolution 14–15, 191
Inn at Whitewell, Clitheroe, Lancashire 45, 47–8, 49
Isle of Purbeck, Dorset 156–9
Isles of Scilly 182–5

Keld & Ravenseat, North Yorkshire 33–6
Kent 230–3
Kettlewell, North Yorkshire 41–2, 44
Kielder Forest, Northumberland 85–8
Kilburn White Horse, North Yorkshire 97–101
Kinder Scout 103, 104, 105–7
Kings Head, Tealby, Lincolnshire 116, 120

Lake District 14, 20–33
Lancashire 14, 15, 37–40, 45–9
Langstrath Country Inn, Stonethwaite, Lake District 20, 21, 22–3
Langwathby, Cumbria 16, 19
Levisham, North Yorkshire 94–6
Lincolnshire 117–24
Lincolnshire Wolds 117–24
Lindisfarne National Nature Reserve 60
Lindisfarne, Northumberland 60–3
Lion Inn, Blakey Ridge, North Yorkshire 89, 90, 92
Logan Rock Inn, Treen, Cornwall 177, 181
Logan Rock, Porth Chapel & Gwennap Head, Cornwall 177–81
Loughrigg Tarn and Terrace, Lake District 24–6
Low Newton-by-the-Sea, Northumberland 68, 71

Melbury Park Estate, Dorset 152–5

Norfolk 192–5
North Cornwall Coast Road 186–
North East of England 58–101
North Pennines 16–19
North West of England 14–57
North York Moors 58, 89–96
North Yorkshire 33–6, 89–101
North Yorkshire Moors Railway 94–5
Northamptonshire 138–41
Northumberland 58, 59, 60–88
Northumberland National Park 58, 76–84

Old Hall Inn, Whitehough, Derbyshire 108, 109, 110–11
Old Nags Head, Edale, Derbyshire 104, 105, 107
Olde Ship Inn, Seahouses, Northumberland 64, 66–7
Oxfordshire 204–8

Pack Horse Inn, Hebden Bridge, West Yorkshire 50, 51–2
Packhorse, South Stoke, Somerset 147, 148, 151
Paper Mill Inn, Whitehough, Derbyshire 108
Peak District 102–3, 104–11
Pennine Way 18, 35–6, 104, 105
Pennines 14, 50, 58
Pheasant Inn, Higher Burwardsley, Cheshire 54, 55, 57
Pheasant Inn, Stannersburn, Northumberland 85, 86, 88
Pigs Nose Inn, East Prawle, Devon 165, 166, 167, 168
Pin Mill & River Orwell Circular, Suffolk 196–9
Playden Oasts Inn, Rye, East Sussex 226, 229
Porthcurno, Cornwall 147, 178–9
Prawle Head, Devon 165–8

Ram Inn, Firle, East Sussex 217, 219, 220
Ravenseat & Keld, North Yorkshire 33–6
Red Lion, Avebury, Wiltshire 142, 144, 145

Ribble Valley, Lancashire 45, 47–9
Ribblehead Viaduct, North Yorkshire 37–40
Rose and Thistle, Alwinton, Northumberland 72, 74–5
Royal Oak, Cardington, Shropshire 125, 128
Rye, East Sussex 190, 226–9

St Agnes Beacon Circular, Cornwall 146, 169–72
St Martin's, Isles of Scilly 182–5
Sandstone Trail, Cheshire/Shropshire 54–7
Scafell Pike from Wasdale Head, Like District 28–32
Sculthorpe Mill, Sculthorpe, Norfolk 192, 193, 195
Seahouses to Bamburgh Circular, Northumberland 64–7
Serpentine Circular, Cornwall 173–6
Settle–Carlisle Railway 37, 39–40
Seven Stones Inn, Isles of Scilly 182, 185
Shepherds Inn, Langwathby, Cumbria 16, 18, 19
Shere, Surrey 191, 209–12
Ship Inn, Lindisfarne, Northumberland 60, 62–3
Ship Inn, Low Newton, Northumberland 68, 71
Shropshire/Shropshire Hills 125–8
Silbury Hill & Avebury, Wiltshire 142–5
Slad/Slad Valley, Stroud, Gloucestershire 134–7
Somerset 147, 148–51
South Downs National Park 190, 213–25
South East England 190–233
South Stoke Circular, Somerset 148–51
South West Coast Path 177, 178–81
South West England 146–89
Square & Compass, Worth Matravers, Dorset 156, 158, 159
Staffordshire 112–16
Stag & Huntsman, Hambledon, Oxfordshire 204, 206, 208
Star Inn, Harbottle, Northumberland 76, 77, 78–9

Station Inn, Ribbleshead, North Yorkshire 37–8, 39–40
Stonethwaite, Lake District 20–3
Suffolk 196–9, 201, 203
Surrey 209–12
Sussex/East Sussex 213–29

Tan Hill Inn, North Yorkshire 14, 33, 35, 36
Tealby Loop, Lincolnshire 117–20
Three Blackbirds, Woodditton, Suffolk 200, 201, 203
Three Horseshoes, Elsted, Sussex 213, 215, 216
Tiger Inn, East Dean, East Sussex 221, 222, 224
Tinners Arms, Zennor, Cornwall 147, 186, 188, 189

Warren House Inn, Dartmoor, Devon 147, 160, 161, 163–4
Wasdale Head Inn, Wasdale, Lake District 28, 31–2
Welsh Marches 103, 125–33
West Yorkshire 50–3
White Horse Inn, Chilham, Kent 230, 231, 232, 233
White Horse, Shere, Surrey 209, 210–11, 212
Wiltshire 142–5
Winspit Quarry Circular, Dorset 156–9
Woolpack Inn, Slad, Gloucestershire 102, 134, 135, 136–7
Worth Matravers & Winspit Quarry, Dorset 156–9

Yew Tree Inn, Cauldron, Staffordshire 103, 112, 115, 116
Yorkshire Dales 33–6, 41–4

Zennor Head Circular, Cornwall 147, 186–9